Medical School 2.0

2.0

AN UNCONVENTIONAL GUIDE TO LEARN FASTER, ACE THE USMLE, AND GET INTO YOUR TOP CHOICE RESIDENCY

By David Larson, MD

To Janna, my muse, my teacher, my best friend.

CONTENTS

SECTION IV: FINE TUNING YOUR LEARNING SYSTEM   107

SECTION V: TESTING—THE FINAL REVIEW AND WHAT TO DO ON TEST DAY   163

Prologue: My Story and Why You Need This Book

I was terrified.

Not only had I taken the bare minimum of college science classes required for medical school, but I had spent the last two years living in Spain and India doing absolutely nothing science related. For years, I had heard horror stories about medical school: "it was the worst 4 years of my life," " I barely had time to sleep or eat," "I survived it, but that was ALL I did."

However, I was in luck—our schedule for our first week had three hours blocked out for a seminar—"How to study in Medical School. I was hoping that here I'd learn some of the tools to succeed.

It was late afternoon on orientation week, my third day of medical school when I walked into McMillan Hall, the classroom that was supposed to be my home for the next several years. A movie theatre-like massive room with stadium seating and continuous curvilinear desks faced the front stage and podium with two massive screens and projectors. The scent of fresh coffee and Red Bull filled the air as all 162 of us shuffled in to hear the best advice of how to learn an absurd amount of information in just four years.

Enter Dr. Jane Talloway (fictional name to preserve anonymity), our PhD learning specialist hired by the USC School of Medicine, whose job it was to teach us how to survive medical school academically. A late 40-something bespectacled heavy-set woman in loose black pants and a purplish-blue blouse, she vaguely resembled Janet Reno.

"Generally, we recommend that you spend at least one half hour per hour of lecture pre-reading the class notes. Then, after lecture, you'll want to spend one-to-two hours per hour of lecture reviewing the material. If you can keep this up on a daily basis, you should do just fine."

As she spoke, I flustered to flip through my schedule for the next few months to see just what this might look like: hmmm... 6-8 hours of lecture a day, that's 3-4 hours of pre-reading the night before, and then 6 16 hours of review that night! At best, this would be a 15 hour work day, probably much longer at first, then add in the drive to and from school, and an hour break for dinner, and that makes a minimum daily schedule of 7AM – 12AM Monday-Friday on school-related activity, with 5-6 hours a night to sleep, talk to friends, exercise, or do anything else non-school related.

A knot began to form and gnarl itself into a heavy ball in my stomach as the hopelessness of this scenario set in. Raw fear bubbled up in my chest like boiling milk overflowing from a too-small pot. My life was over.

My eyes glazed over as I completely zoned out of whatever Dr. Talloway was saying next... I was terrified and furious—was she joking about this? This is impossible! I can't survive this! Should I just drop out now? This is just evil!
Gone were the days of surfing every day. No more hobbies or exercise at all actually, no possibility of exploring the amazing night-life in LA, no more concerts, definitely no more traveling—I guess life as I knew it really was over. But I really did want to be a doctor; I loved learning the sciences, and above all wanted to help people in a tangible and direct way.

As I drove home that night, I started problem solving. There had to be a better way. I knew I would die a bit inside if I had to put aside all my other interests and life outside of medical school for four years, so I made a deal with myself—I would try it out for a few months, and search constantly for a better way, and if I had found nothing and was continuing to die inside from this inhuman schedule, I'd drop out and pursue something else...It wasn't worth killing myself to help others.

I started just like everyone else, because I didn't know there was another way...Here's what a typical day looked like:

6:00 AM: Alarm goes off, I'm still exhausted so hit the snooze button.

6:45 AM: Eventually get out of bed after multiple angry snoozes. Shower and grab coffee

7:20 AM: Leave for school, and sit in LA traffic listening to music, thinking I should have gotten up earlier to pre-read for today's lectures.

8:00 – 4:00: Lectures, in 50-minute blocks with an hour break for lunch. Each hour has its own set of lecture notes and PowerPoint slides. I arrive at my first lecture 10 minutes late. Sit in the back with my friends, open up the laptop, vaguely pay attention while I continue to wake up, check email, check the news, laugh with my buddies about the party last weekend. I take some scant notes while I am paying attention, feeling productive that I'm there at class, and knowing it's ok if I don't "get it" all now. I'll have plenty of time later to understand the material.

4:20 PM: Drive home, again in traffic, listening to music.

5:00 PM – 11:00 PM: Study at home or in the library, cooking dinner somewhere in between. I'd re-read the lecture notes and highlight them, sometimes taking notes in the margin and do the same for the PowerPoint slides. I'd find myself zoning out a lot while studying and inevitably get caught up in random conversations with my roommates to distract myself.

11:00 – 1:00 AM: Wind down before bed and do it all over again.

Yet even studying this much, I still wasn't even close to having a command of the material we were supposed to be learning. I felt like I had a mild grasp on it but in no way was I satisfied with how well I knew the material.

The week before the test, my roommates and I would start stressing out and cramming... studying the lecture notes in a haphazard way, making our own notes, reading over some review books, but we weren't sure which books to read, as there were so many that were "recommended reading." There was WAY more material than I could ever memorize, so I just tried my best to guess what was most important and focus on that. No exercising, no going out, just 18 hour days of studying, commuting, and test prep.

Test Day: I feel exhausted and kind of prepared, but far from where I imagined I'd be. I make it through the test, vaguely feeling familiar with all the concepts on the test, but in no way on top of it. I get a 78%, which is fine since a passing grade is anything above 70%.

This is how things went for my first block, "Core 1". The material was actually very interesting and fun to learn in small doses... so is eating ice cream, but to eat Ben and Jerry's for every meal every day would get old very fast... Life at this time was one-dimensional and overwhelming, but it was more or less what I expected from medical school from the stories I had heard. I was losing faith that this was the right choice for me and yet continued to be determined to find a better way.

And so my search began...as the weeks and months rolled on, I interviewed hundreds of medical students and recently graduated physicians. I spent countless hours scouring online forums for best practices. I bought every book I could find on studying in med school, and studying in general, always trying out every strategy I heard about in order to find the best way to succeed in medical school while still having a healthy life.

I tried taking notes in a bunch of different ways and making notes of those notes. I tried making flashcards. I tried getting copies of the smartest student's notes. I tried webcasting at double speed. I tried watching online videos. I tried reading review books. I tried audio books...I lived my academic life as an experiment, constantly testing people's recommendations for studying and then trying to improve upon them.

This investment began to pay dividends very quickly and the results were far greater than I could have ever imagined. I couldn't' believe it... After about 3 months of putting the best practices to use, my time spent on school kept on getting smaller and smaller, and my grades went up and up. And this trend continued on and on... There seemed to be no end to how far this process could go. On top of that, studying actually became a lot of fun. I woke up in the morning excited to learn and study that day. I focused better than ever before and soon was able to focus in nearly any environment. I was able to channel the passion I had for the human sciences without getting overwhelmed by having too much of it. Other students started to notice and began to ask me for advice, and I started teaching others. By the end of my second year, I had trimmed Dr. Talloway's suggested 15-23 hour workday to 2-3 hours a day. I had more free time than I knew what to do with—time to surf and play the guitar, time to cook dinners with friends, go to concerts, read novels, do whatever I wanted! While in "school" I was able to spend weeks in Nicaragua learning about healthcare in a developing country and surfing world-class waves, in Guatemala helping to treat and prevent Xeroderma Pigmentosum, a rare genetic disease, a trip to Europe with my girlfriend, and learning about infectious diseases and hiking the Inca trail in Peru. I was able to be student body president of the school, work in jails to prevent gang-related violence and drug use, and help start a global health program.

I did all this while achieving the highest possible academic honors in medical school, achieving in the top 99.7th percentile on the USMLE Steps 1 and 2, our nation-wide licensing exams, being initiated into Alpha Omega Alpha honor society, receiving over a dozen merit-based scholarships, and having the doors open to pretty much any residency I wanted to do. I not only was able to perform on tests, but my long-term retention of the material I had learned was greater than I could have ever imagined. And while doing all this, I had a magnificent time in the PROCESS, I LOVED medical school and will remember those days as some of the best in my life.

I have written this book because I know without a doubt that the processes and principles behind my success can be LEARNED and REPLICATED (and improved upon even more by you!) I am not a genius and I don't have a photographic memory. Compared with my peers in medical school, I got sub-par grades on my SAT's and MCAT, below average grades in college, and worked just as hard as everyone else for many years. Yet, after learning many of these study skills and techniques, I feel like a genius.

Using feedback from other students, I've spent hundreds of hours refining and perfecting the study and learning strategies in this book and have distilled this knowledge into a set of easily digestible principles to teach to you. I know they work because I've taught them to many other students who experienced nearly identical success stories. Students kept asking me to write these down into a book, and now in the later years of my residency I've finally had more time to do just that.

In Medical School there are great review books and summary books for information but very few resources that teach how to must effectively transfer the information in the books into our brains.

While the principles discussed in this book are designed with medical students in mind, it's concepts, principles, and strategies are applicable to all students of science. That means everyone from high school students in AP Biology to pre-med students interested in medicine, to nursing and pharmacy students, Physician Assistant and Physical Therapy Students, to residents preparing for the USMLE Step III, to practicing physicians preparing to re-board in their specialty. The strategies work best for students in memorization-intensive fields who need to learn a large amount of objective information and retain it well, and who want to spend minimal time doing this.

These learning strategies work well not only for mastering your core material but also work incredibly well for preparing for tests. Some students use these methods only for test-prep for the USMLE Step 1 and 2 and for their 3rd year shelf exams, while others will use it for their core course material in addition to exams.

Regardless of where you are, or whatever your situation is, you can start putting these tools to practice to dramatically increase your results AND free time. After about 6 weeks of using these strategies, most students achieve most if not all of the following results:

- Spending MUCH less time on learning-related activities = MORE FREE TIME (Expect a 50% - 500% reduction in your time spent learning).

- Better grades (Expect to increase at least one letter grade. For example, if you averaged 75% on tests, expect at least 85%).

- Lasting learning: Expect to be able to recall and remember the material you learned almost naturally with minimal review (that means less time needed to study for tests, or to review when you're on the wards seeing patients).

- More fun while learning: You may think that these words never belong in the same sentence, but for now just trust me that it might be possible to actually look forward to studying, enjoying both the process of mastering your material, as well as your ample free time.

- Mastery of a set of study strategies that you can continue to use throughout the rest of your life and apply to a wide variety of fields.

Most books on learning and studying are not only targeted to high school students and college students, but are written by PhD educational psychologists who often are many years away from the actual classroom experience. Often, some of these ideas make sense in theory, but when you try to put these principles to use, they don't actually work. Then there are a few books out there about medical school specifically, but they mainly focus on how to get in and on brief overviews of all the aspects of medical school, leaving you few practical tools to put into practice.

This material will be exactly what the others aren't—Practical. This book contains my hundreds of hours of trial and error, interviews and advice from over 100 other highly successful medical students and physicians, all combined with some of the latest findings in the neuroscience of learning, to give you a menu of ways to study so that you can get the best results from your precious time.

The book begins with the foundation, in which I'll go through some basic principles you'll need to understand before moving on. After this, you'll find six distinct sections covering the core material.

Section 1: Defining Success: In this section, we'll go over your goals for school itself and for your overall life within school. In order to get the top results that you want in medical school, it's important to get clear about what you really want from the medical school experience AND to get clear about how you want to spend all that new free time you're going to have!

Section 2: Choosing What to Learn: How to Turn Sludge into Evian: Here, we'll go over how to identify and choose top quality learning sources, regardless of what you're studying for.

Section 3: Learning 2.0: In this section, we'll go over some of the basics of neuroscience as it relates to learning and memory. We'll then talk about why the way most people study doesn't make sense after knowing this, and then I'll teach you a step-by-step study system that makes use of the latest findings in neuroscience to supercharge your learning potential.

Section 4: Fine Tuning Your Learning System: Here, we'll go over some of the other details of optimal learning— where to study, when to study, how long, with whom, and what to eat and drink to supercharge your brain.

Section 5: Testing—The Final Review and What To Do on Test Day: In this final section, we'll go over detailed tips for how to review material you've already learned and how to prepare for and take tests optimally.

The material in this book is designed to be simple and easy to understand, yet also comprehensive so you have all your questions answered. To help with this, I've also included detailed screencast videos that cover every aspect of the study tools, so you can have an over-the-shoulder experience of what it looks like to put these tools into practice. You can access these at my website www.facebook.com/studycoachmd.

I created this book to not only help you succeed with your learning goals, but also to help you do this in minimal time and all the while ENJOYING the time you spend doing it—yes, you can have your cake and eat it too.

I hope you find as much value as I did from these techniques and that you use them for the rest of your lives, to not only stay atop of the ever-expanding field of medicine in your specialty, but also to create an incredible life while doing so!

-Dave Larson, M.D.

Foundation:

This section is here to teach you about some of the basic principles that this book is based upon. Before getting into the nitty gritty details, this section will help you zoom out and reflect to get into the right mindset for approaching this book.

Rather than repeat the same principles over and over, I'll try to cover them clearly and briefly here so that we're on the same page when we get started.
Take some time to reflect on these ideas as you go through them, and feel free to refer back to this section throughout the book as needed.

Principle 1: A Learning System vs. a Learning Source

For most people, the source of information they use to learn medicine is the curriculum provided by their school. And this makes a lot of sense, your school has spent a lot of time and money designing a curriculum that covers what you need to know to be a competent doctor and pass the national licensing exams. Taken as a whole, the curriculum, including your lectures, lecture notes, PowerPoint slides, labs, and recommended reading consist of a very large learning SOURCE.

When most people try to make studying easier, they try to invent a better learning SOURCE—one that can improve upon some aspect of the information you're getting. For example, the team at First Aid found a way to consolidate the best information from lecture notes and textbooks into a very high quality set of information that covers the basic detail of what students need to know to do well on the USMLE Step 1.
Kaplan and Princeton Review do the same thing, creating their

own course content, bringing in their own expert teachers, to present you with better information. Companies like USMLE World go a step further in not only giving you information, but also giving it to you in a unique way (practice test questions in this case).

There are literally hundreds of these types of books and as you go along in your training, you'll discover more and more. However, at the end of the day, each of these represent different standardized learning SOURCES. These review books are important, and I definitely recommend using some of the best ones as you study because they'll save you A LOT of time.

However, what they're missing is your own unique individuality. None of us are the exact same, and we all have slightly different learning needs, strengths, and weaknesses. There is no way a particular learning source, whether it's a medical school curriculum or a review book, can cover all of your own unique learning needs. This is why when you ask friends what the best books are; you'll inevitably get a variety of answers.

Furthermore, these tools tell you little to nothing about HOW to study them. At the end of the day, you will probably still be using your old way of studying but with newer and better books. This is the equivalent of giving an amateur chef the best ingredients in the world—if he doesn't have great cooking skills to begin with, the dinner isn't going to be world-class even if the ingredients are great. On the other hand, if you put a top chef in an average kitchen, she will likely be able to create something spectacular. This book will train you to be such a chef. It's about training you to understand and effectively use a learning SYSTEM that can be applied to ANY SOURCE of information. Where a learning SOURCE describes "what" you'll learn, a learning SYSTEM teaches "how" to learn that information. When you master the "how" of learning combined with the best sources of information, you'll be on your way to becoming a master learner.

Learning a new way of approaching and learning information will take some time to get used to, but this is an investment worth making. As you get familiar with this learning system and put the tools to practice, you'll not only see results right away, but also you'll eventually engrain the learning system into your long-term memory so that it becomes a habit. This means that regardless of what learning demands you face in the future, be it a national exam like the MCAT, or USMLE, or a third-year rotation and shelf exam, or an organ system, or even your specialty boards, you will have tools that you can apply to ANY sources of information to maximize your personal yield out of each source.

Now more than ever, medicine is changing rapidly. Rather than invest your time in finding the best source to learn the current information, you're much better off spending your time learning how to learn, a system of learning anything that you can use for the rest of your medical career!
The goal is YOUR personal best—to maximize the potential of your own unique mind and apply it to learn in record time with record results. Enjoy the ride!

4

Principle 2: Enjoy the Process

My mom sent me this amazing anonymous quote while I was an undergrad, and it still affects me to this day...

> *"We convince ourselves that life will be better after we get married, have a baby, then another. Then we're frustrated that the kids aren't old enough and we'll be more content when they are. After that, we're frustrated that we have teenagers to deal with. We'll certainly be happy when they're out of that stage. We tell ourselves that our life will be complete when our spouse gets his or her act together, when we get a nicer car, are able to go on a nice vacation, when we retire. The truth is, there's no better time to be happy than right now. If not now, when? Your life will always be filled with challenges. It's best to admit this to yourself and decide to be happy anyway...*
>
> *There is no way to happiness. Happiness is the way. So, treasure every moment that you have and treasure it more because you shared it with someone special, special enough to spend your time with...and remember that time waits for no one.*
>
> *So, stop waiting until you finish school, until you go back to school, until you lose ten pounds, until you gain ten pounds, until you have kids, until your kids leave the house, until you start work, until you retire, until you get married, until you get divorced, until Friday night, until Sunday morning, until you get a new car or home, until your car or home is paid off, until spring, until summer, until fall, until winter, until you're off welfare, until the first or fifteenth, until your song comes on, until you've had a drink, until you've sobered up, until you die, until you're born again to decide that there is no better time than right now to be happy."*
>
> -Anonymous

This quote profoundly affected me since the first time I read it. I suppose it expresses something we all know or at least have thought about before but it so easily slips away—that "happiness is a journey, not a destination." This is especially true for those of us pursuing a career in medicine. It's all too easy to have the mindset that "I'll just get through this, and then relax once I get into residency." Unfortunately, the steps only continue, and after residency there is fellowship, and then getting a job, and then becoming a partner or professor, and the quest can go on and on.

The alternative is to develop the skills NOW to enjoy the PROCESS itself. Yes, it will be a long journey, but it's well worth it, and if you learn how to take care of yourself and have fun WHILE going through the learning experiences, you'll not only do better, but you'll look back on these years as some of the best in your life.

A recent study published in the Journal of Personality and Social Psychology[1] examined nearly a half million people from 63 countries asking the question of what determines happiness. The authors found that it wasn't the level of money that determined one's happiness, but rather an individual's autonomy—their ability to make choices to do what they want, when they want to do it, how they want to do it.

This book is about creating autonomy in your life as a student. You will be empowered with mindsets and tools to completely customize your study experience to be perfect for YOU. You'll also be able to create more free time than you could have ever imagined, giving you even more autonomy to do whatever you like.

---

[1] Wealth and happiness across the world: Material prosperity predicts life evaluation, whereas psychosocial prosperity predicts positive feeling. Diener, Ed; Ng, Weiting; Harter, James; Arora, Raksha. Journal of Personality and Social Psychology, Vol 99(1), Jul 2010, 52-61.

Principle 3: Think Different

"Problems cannot be solved at the same level of awareness that created them."

– Albert Einstein

"It isn't what we don't know that gives us trouble, it's what we know that ain't so"

–Will Rogers

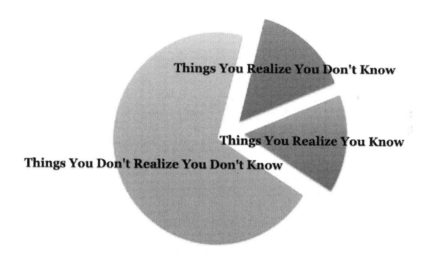

If this pie chart represents everything that exists, the information in most people's conscious awareness comes from our own lives, shaped by our family, our culture, and the unique experiences we've had. While in school, most students spend their time trying to move information from the red wedge to the green wedge, not even aware of the HUGE yellow piece of the pie representing what they don't know they don't know.

When we can get aware of this big slice of life, our minds open to the fact that there may be possibilities out there that we can't even conceive of. This is the attitude of mind that I want you to have as you approach this book. By being comfortable with these as-yet undefined possibilities, you'll be amazed at the solutions that will show up.

I'll be asking you to use this s out-of-the-box type of thinking throughout the book. The most COMMON way to do anything, medical school included, is rarely the most EFFECTIVE way. We're not going to spend much time looking at the center of the bell-shaped-curve of studying, instead, we're going to look at the extreme outliers, the study methods that may seem strange, but that work the best. To achieve extraordinary results from the time you spend learning, you're going to have to think extraordinarily.

All of the study methods in this book have come from students who have taken a risk to do something different. True, many of these techniques turned out to be failures, but some worked very VERY well. This book is a distillation of these highly effective techniques, and it is my hope that you will take it a step further, thinking even further outside of the box, to further improve on these techniques and make them even better for yourself!

Principle 4: Ignore the Crowd

"Whenever you find yourself on the side of the majority, it's time to pause and reflect."

– Mark Twain

Piggybacking on the last principle, this one is about trusting yourself and having the courage to do things your way, even if no one else is doing it.

For example, in undergrad, I found myself just too overworked and stressed out by trying to finish up all the pre-med classes in time to take the MCAT my junior year. I didn't like the competitiveness and the constant sense of urgency. But this is what everyone else was doing, so it had to be the only way, right?

Wrong. When I took a step back and really thought about what I cared about, I realized I was in it for the long haul, that I'm in no rush to go to med school right away, and that I'd much rather enjoy my time in college at a slower pace even if it meant I'd have a year off before going to med school. So I slowed everything down. I let the competitive people run right past me, "winning" the race. In fact, I exited the race all-together. Everyone thought I was nuts and was making a HUGE mistake, but I did my best to ignore them. It paid off, big time. I only took one or two tough pre-med classes a semester and had loads of free time to enjoy college life. I liked it so much, I ended up taking 2 years off before starting med school to travel the world and to live and teach in Spain. I haven't regretted it for a day.

This same process has happened for me over and over again and has become easier and easier each time. It's not about always doing what the crowd is not doing, because sometimes the crowd will be doing it the best way for you, but it's about having the bottom line be about what YOU want regardless of what people around you say. Everyone is going to have advice and an opinion about what you're doing, whether you ask for it or not. Most of these opinions are based on their own fears and worries and wanting to justify their way of doing it. If your peers see you hiking the trails in Yosemite while they're pulling 16 hour days studying, they're gonna be jealous and pissed off. No doubt they'll criticize your way of studying, telling you it won't work, or you're wasting your tuition money, or whatever else. But at the end of the day, what matters is what you want and what works. If their advice sounds good, try it out and see for yourself if it works. This is exactly what I want you to do with the tools I am going to teach you in this book. Don't believe anything I say, but DO think about it and try it out, and see if the results work for you.

Principle 5: Ask for Exceptions

It's ok to break the rules. Sometimes the rules are there as general guidelines, and if you have an idea that honors the intention of the rules, usually the powers that be will let you do it your way as long as you don't tell others about it. Most people don't even think it's an option to ask for exceptions, and if they do, they rarely have the courage to pull the trigger, afraid of the potential consequences. At the end of the day though, there really are no consequences. You have NOTHING to loose by asking for what you want. Sure, you may not get it (most of the time you probably will), but at least you asked.

For example, how could Harvard medical student (now a famous international health physician) Paul Farmer spend ALL of his time in Haiti, flying back to Boston once every couple of months for tests, missing dozens of MANDATORY meetings and classes? Simple—he asked the Dean for a special exception to the rules, and he got it.

In my own life in medical school, I've asked for countless exceptions, and most of the time got them. For example, I was able to take weeks off of school, missing "required" classes to volunteer in Central America. In applying for scholarships and grants, if I were past the deadline, I'd ask for a special extension—and most of the time, I would get it.

12

Principle 6: Maximize the Mandatory

You won't always be able to get your special exceptions, and at times, you will have to participate in mandatory activities, and just do it. Sometimes it's just not worth it to fight the establishment, even if some of the activities don't make sense. In this case, you want to do whatever is in your power to turn the requirement into something useful.

Because potential options are basically limitless, this process will be much easier after completing section I, when you have a clear idea about what you want.

For example, let's say you don't learn very well from lectures, but for a certain system, lectures are required at your school. In this case, you'll want to maximize the time you spend in those lectures so you're getting the most yield from them that you can. Details of just how to do this will be laid out later in the book.

14

Principle 7: Lessons from an Italian Economist: Pareto's Principle

Vilfredo Pareto was an Italian Economist born in the late 1800s, who noticed that 80% of the land in Italy was owned by only 20% of the population... He later noticed that in his household garden, 80% of his produce of peas came from only 20% of his plants. Interesting.... Could this be applied to other areas of life?

Indeed it can, "Pareto's Principle," commonly known as the 80/20 rule has been applied for decades in many fields—from business to software, from mathematics to politics. The basic rule of thumb is that 80% of the outputs come from 20% of the inputs.

I first learned of Pareto from Tim Ferris in his book *The Four Hour Workweek*, and applying this principle in my own life changed things forever. 20% of the things I owned gave me 80% of my satisfaction from material goods. 20% of my friends fulfilled 80% of my social connection needs, 20% of the food in my fridge and cupboards gave me 80% of my enjoyment of food. And so on, and so forth...
This principle can just as easily be applied to learning in medical school. I encourage you to think about it with each section we go through, and refer back to this foundation if you need a refresher.

The goal is to initially focus ONLY on that 20%, and ELIMINATE the other 80%. Yes, I know you want more than an 80% on your test, but as you continue to apply this rule and focus down onto only the most essential things, your results are going to increase exponentially, giving you clarity about your next steps to achieve your peak performance goals.

Section I: Defining Success

I bet many of you were voted "Most Likely to Succeed" at some point in your life. But what exactly does that mean? Make a ton of money? Have a ton of degrees? Have a lot of political power? Have a loving marriage? Be a good parent? Run a non-profit organization?

Success is such an overused term, and it means so many different things to different people. And to complicate matters even further, many people in your life, while they may not be able to define what success means for them, will each have their own definition of what success means for YOU.

For your parents, it may mean getting a great job after medical school. For your professor, it may mean developing a deep-seeded passion for their field. For your principle investigator, it may mean doing cutting-edge research, while for your friends it may mean making life-long memories and bonds to last a lifetime. This list is endless, and to try to shape your own definition of success form this list is nearly impossible and not very helpful.

At the end of the day, the person that matters most in this equation is YOU, and it's YOUR definition of a successful student that we're going to focus on.
Also, it's beyond the scope of this book to focus on what it means to be a successful person, that's a much bigger task. For now, we're going to focus on what it means to be a success in medical school. We'll look at your goals, your values, your dreams, your hopes, your fantasies, and a lot more to arrive at a clear picture of what YOU want to get out of your medical school experience.

Vary rarely do students directly reflect on the question of what success means to them. As a result, they often get lost in other people's definitions of success, never quite achieving all of them, and as a result feeling in many senses like a failure. This creates a downward spiral of low-self esteem, lowered productivity, and sub-par results.

On the other hand, if you define specific goals that, once achieved, would satisfy your own definition of academic success, you could start an upward spiral of feeling energized, enthusiastic, and hopeful that you can achieve anything you desire. Not only does this feel good, but it also will help you to study and learn MUCH more effectively.

This book is about YOU. It's about customization the medical school experience to achieve and go far beyond your goals in record time. Naturally, the first step is becoming aware of the goals that meet your definition of success. This will both give you energy to propel you through your studies and help clarify what you want to do with all your newly created free time.

By the end of this section, you will have a broader understanding and clear definition of what success means both within and out of medical school. You will have a simple and clear list of personalized goals to focus and fuel you as you forge ahead.

Chapter 1: Goals for Medical School

There are many different reasons people go to medical school. Some are clear from day one that they want to be a surgeon. Others simply want to help people in a tangible way but aren't sure which specialty they want to pursue; some envision a life of service in the developing world, while others envision a life of research and teaching. There are even some who will only get their MD's for credibility and then work in business or politics. Regardless of your own motivation, the clearer you are about your own personal goals for going to medical school, the better you'll be able to design your own curriculum and study systems to accomplish them.

These goals are not only about the big picture of what you want to do after medical school, but also describe your ideal scenario for day-to-day experience while still IN medical school. For example, here were some of my goals for school:

- Learn the medical sciences well with high long-term retention so that I can apply what I've learned practically to my future patients.
- Get into my TOP CHOICE residency in the SPECIALTY and CITY that I want.
- Learn how to be an effective life-long learner—develop study and time management skills that I can use forever as I stay on top of my chosen field.
- Practice what I preach—that is, to take care of my body and mind to embody the health that I'm teaching to my patients.
- Create plenty of free time to do things I enjoy outside of school.
- Have a blast—Enjoying BOTH my free time AND my time spent learning.
- Create life-long friendships, spending plenty of quality-time with my friends.
- Develop a solid network of colleagues, professors, and researchers to collaborate with in the future.

- Learn how to budget my money and understand the financial system of loans, loan-repayment, taxes, and options for minimizing my debt.

As you can see, this isn't rocket-science, and it doesn't have to be hard to think of these goals. They don't necessarily have to be realistic at this point. In fact, it's better that they DON'T seem realistic. In this initial step, it's important to DREAM BIG, and put in writing everything you want for yourself, regardless of whether it's "possible" or not. I think many med students would agree that my above list would be impossible in medical school. I thought so too at first, and it turns out it was easily achievable, but I wouldn't have know this when I started.

Process: Discovering Your Goals for Medical School

This is not meant to be a comprehensive review of your goals but rather a quick way to jump-start your mind into dreaming big and getting an idea of your own personal goals. You'll find that after doing this, your mind will get rolling on these ideas, and you'll get more and more clear as the weeks roll on— bringing more and more of your dreams and hopes into focus. Lets get started.

Instructions:

Before moving on, set aside 20-30 minutes of time where you will not be interrupted and where you can reflect in peace to free-write on the questions below. This means you sit with pen-in-hand, or hands on keyboard, focus on the question, and write without stopping. If your mind is thinking, "I have no idea what success is," then write that. If you're thinking, "I need to pick up my dry-cleaning later today," then write that too. The point is to write continuously to overcome your mind's tendency to avoid the difficult questions.

1. Why did I decide to go to medical school?
2. What do I want to get out of school?
3. If I achieved X, Y, Z, I could reflect back on my time in school and KNOW it was a great success.
4. What's the best-case scenario I can imagine for myself at school? What would a perfect day look like? Dream BIG!

Great job! For now, put this list aside, we'll come back to it later.

Chapter 2: Big Picture Life Goals

You are more than a medical student. You are an extraordinary human being with your own unique hopes and dreams. These dreams are what make you, you. These are the things that EXCITE you, the things that INSPIRE you, the things that keep you up at night.

It is INTEGRAL that you take the time to reflect on these big dreams because these are the things that are going to motivate you to create the free time you need to be whole. No one was born to only be a medical student, yet the system is designed to be so difficult that many students do just this. I want to help you keep all of your passions alive and have the time to thrive in medical school academically while still pursuing your overall life dreams.

My friend Shahin wants to be a kidney surgeon AND a screenwriter. Who says he can't do both? He got his first script published in INTERNSHIP, and continues to write scripts as a laparoscopic kidney transplant fellow. Another friend, Ari, inspired by Paul Farmer (if you don't know who this is, PLEASE read the book Mountains beyond Mountains ASAP), wanted to create his own innovative malaria treatment and prevention program in West Africa. He did, raising over a million dollars and recruiting a treatment and volunteer team of over 100 people while a student at Harvard Med! Michael Crichton wrote Andromeda strain while in medical school, 'nuff said.

While this book is focused mainly on your school goals, it is also focused on getting you plenty of free time to achieve the larger life goals outside of school. When you are crystal clear about how you're going to use all your free time, you'll be motivated to stay focused and on track to create that free time.

So let's get started! Because these goals can be a lot more diverse and cover a much broader territory than just medical school, I find it useful to separate them into what you want to DO, BE, and HAVE (Props to Tim Ferris[2] for this idea).

Here are some examples of my own life goals:

DO

- Trek the Inca Trail in Peru
- Scuba Dive in Belize
- Go Wine Tasting in South Africa
- Meditate in Bhutan
- Skydive out of a Helicopter in Interlaken, Switzerland
- Meet Paul Farmer
- Start a public health NGO in the developing world.
- Start a vaccination campaign for Mexican children in Tijuana, funded by school donations.

BE

- A Great Doctor
- A Loving Husband
- A Supportive Dad
- A Great Surfer
- A Writer
- Fluent in French

HAVE
- A 3-bedroom house within walking distance to a beach with great surfing in Southern California.
- A thriving medical practice in the city of my dreams.
- A Toyota Prius
- A quiver of at least 4 surfboards for all occasions
- A new MacBook Pro

---

2 Ferriss, T (2007). The 4-Hour Workweek. New York, NY: Crown Publishing Group.

Notice how some of these goals are very specific (i.e. the house), and some are more general (i.e. be a "writer"). You many not know anything more than the generalities at this point, but the eventual goal is to be as specific as possible. The more you can see, taste, touch, smell, and feel your dreams, the more likely you are to accomplish them.

Process: Brainstorming Your Life Goals

Just as we did above with your goals for medical school, I want you to take at least 20-30 minutes to free-write on the following questions, separating your responses in terms of DO, BE, HAVE.

1. What are your lifelong dreams?
2. What EXCITES you?
3. If you had 10 billion dollars in the bank, what would you buy? What would you do?
4. If you could literally design your dream life, what would it look like? Take me through a day in impeccable detail (i.e. where do you wake up, how do you wake up (alarm clock, sunlight, kiss from your significant other), what does the room look like, what do you do next, what do you have for breakfast, who cooks it, etc.... the more detail, the more senses involved, the more you FEEL it, the better!)

Great! Again, put this list aside with the other one, we'll come back to it later.

Chapter 3: Wordsmithing

To make these goals as effective as possible, it is important to make sure they are written in the clearest way possible to help you accomplish them. According to recent research[3] in goal setting, there are certain ways of wording goals, or "key performance indicators," to make them more likely to be accomplished. The following points summarize these characteristics:

- **Specific**: As I mentioned earlier, the more specific the goal, the better. Instead of "I am a good guitar player," say I can play this and that song flawlessly without reading the music.

- **Measurable**: It is important to have an unambiguous description of the goal so that you know whether or not it has been completed. For example, instead of "I get a great score on Step I," you might say "I get at least a 240 on the USMLE Step I." This way, an objective observer can say without a doubt whether or not you accomplished this.

- **Positively Stated**: Make sure the goal describes something you DO want, not what you DON'T Want. Usually, you can just use the opposite of what you don't want to figure this out. For example, if a goal was I Don't Want to Fail Biochemistry, switch it to I DO want to pass Biochemistry (or better yet, I DO want to get an A+ in Biochemistry!)

- **Achievable by YOU**: By this I mean, that the goal is within YOUR control. Instead of a goal of "a cute girl asks me out on a date," the goal might be "I ask a cute

---

[3] Meyer, Paul J (2003). "What would you do if you knew you couldn't fail? Creating S.M.A.R.T. Goals". Attitude Is Everything: If You Want to Succeed Above and Beyond. Meyer Resource Group, Incorporated, The.

girl on a date." This way it's up to me to ask her on a date, she may say no which is out of my control, but it's totally within my power to at least ask her.

- **Action Oriented**: It is important for your written goals to focus on an action. This especially applies to all the goals we put in the "BE" column. For example, take my goal of being a writer. The do part of this might be, I write a book and submit it for publishing, or even something as simple as I write for 2 hours once a week. As another example, a goal of "I am fluent in French" might transform to, I carry on a 10-minute conversation in French.

- **Present Tense**: It can seem confusing at first to write a goal in the present tense. For example, if I am a first year medical student, and my goal is to do well on the USMLE Step 1, I might at first write "I will get at least a 255 on the USMLE Step 1." After all, I haven't taken the exam yet, so wording it in the future is correct. For grammar classes, yes, but not for goal setting. When setting goals, you want to write your goal in the present tense AS IF it has already been accomplished. This is because our minds don't like unresolved conflicts, also known as "cognitive dissonance," and whenever there is such a dispute, our minds will work tirelessly to resolve the conflict. We can use this natural tendency to our advantage to accomplish our goals. For example, let's say that right now I only have about 1 hour of free time each day, but my goal is to have at least 6 hours. I might then write my goal something like "I now have at least 6 hours of free time each day." While not at all true in the moment, it sets up an unconscious "cognitive dissonance" that our mind will try to resolve by either by telling you "no you don't, you only have 1 hour of free time" (note—this is not the option we'll be choosing), or by helping you to find a creative way to create at least 6 hours of free time each day.

Note, you may not be able to, or want to, apply all these characteristics to your goals, and they may not fit with some goals such as "I feel happy while I study" because these are subjective by nature. The point is to have an awareness of these characteristics and to apply them where you can to your goals. At the end of the day, you want your goals to FEEL empowering, motivating, and clear to you.

Let's look at some examples of well-formed goals that might apply to you.

Medical School Goals

- I have at least 6 hours of free time each day to do whatever I want while still getting "honors" on all my rotations.
- I feel happy and productive while I am learning.
- I now have a score of at least a 250 of the USMLE Step 1 Exam.
- I remember my basic sciences so well that I don't have to study in order to apply them to patients I see clinically in my third year.

Broader Life Goals

- I spend at least 1 week surfing in Costa Rica
- I volunteer at least 1 weekend giving vaccinations to children in Mexico.
- I write at least 2 hours each week on a book idea I have.
- I have a 2012 black Toyota Prius.
- I initiate a conversation with a girl I'm attracted to at least twice a week (this might be a first step toward the overall goal of being a husband if I'm currently single).

Process: Refining Your Goals

Now, take out the goals you made earlier, and again, before moving on, set aside 20-30 minutes of uninterrupted time to wordsmith your goals. As you look at your goals, consider the following questions:

- **Specific**: As yourself what EXACTLY you are referring to, being as concrete as possible. This is easiest done with goals of things you want, such as 2013 M6 BMW Convertible, as opposed to a "nice car." It may be more difficult if your goal is a subjective thing such as "feeling happy while I study."

- **Measurable**: Would someone else be able to tell you if your goal is accomplished or not? For example, if your goal is getting "honors" in at least 3 of your third year clerkships, then anyone could easily look at your grades and tell if you did this or not, as opposed to a goal saying "do well in my 3rd year." With subjective goals, such as "I feel happy while I study," try to use wording that would make it clear and easy for you to judge whether you are accomplishing this or not. You might change it to, "I can look back on at least 3 study sessions a week and honestly say I enjoyed my time."

- **Positively Stated**: If you see the words "don't" then re-write it so that you choose the opposite. Instead of "I don't want to study alone" you might write, "I want to study with friends at least 3 days per week."

- **Achievable by YOU**: If there is any part of your goal that depends on someone else doing something, either take it out, or re-word it so that you focus on YOUR part.

- **Action Oriented**: For all your goals in the "BE" column, think about what actions embody that statement. For example, if you wrote, "I am fluent in French" think about what actionable task, if accomplished, would be evidence that you are indeed fluent in French. For example, you might write "I can carry on a 10 minute conversation in French with a stranger" if that would meet your definition of being "fluent" in French.

- **Present Tense**: To the extent you can, write your goal in the present tense, "as if" you already accomplished it.

If you find that you have too many goals, think about applying Pareto's principle to them, so that you get the most bang for your buck. For example, which 20% of hobbies give you 80% of your satisfaction? Which 20% of friends give you 80% of your fun and connection? Which 20% of your workout activities give you 80% of the results you're looking for? As you think about the most valuable 20%, choose these ones for now; knowing you can always change your goals later on.

After refining and wordsmithing your goals, write down (or type out) a polished version that can fit on a single piece of paper, and keep this in a highly visible place, so that you can see it at least once a day, ideally before you start to study. Some good ideas are the bathroom mirror, in the shower, on the steering wheel of your car, or as the background of your computer.

Keep in mind that this doesn't have to be a final draft, if fact, it probably will continue to be refined often, because you've now begun a brainstorming process that will continue to develop as you accomplish these goals and make new ones! The point is that you get in the habit of keeping your attention on these goals daily, because they will help to focus your attention, and will draw you closer and closer to where you want to be.

Congratulations! You just accomplished perhaps the most difficult part of the book. By starting to get clear about what you value and what you want to create in your life in medical school and beyond, you are setting up a strong foundation from which to build your experience over the next several years. If you haven't yet done the processes from this section, I strongly recommend completing them before moving on, because we will continue to come back to this material throughout the book. However, once you have your personal goals in hand, you will be able to use this to guide and direct HOW you use the rest of the material from the book to ACCOMPLISH these goals in record time!

Section II:
Choosing What to Learn:
How to Turn Sludge Into Evian

Several years ago, I was at a TED MED conference where ultra-inventor, Dean Kamen introduced one of his latest inventions—the vapor compression distiller, capable of turning ANY liquid into pure water. Kamen claims it could turn oceans, poisons, even a 50-gallon drum of human urine into clean, tasty H20. If it pans out, and is implemented in the developing world, the hope is that it could wipe out "50% of human disease."

So why is this relevant to us? While I don't have such a machine, we're going to use the same concept to create a process to filter a massive plethora of learning sources (i.e. books, lecture slides, notes) into a very small quantity of the highest quality information. Even if you have the best chef in the world, if her ingredients suck, she won't be able to make a delicious meal. Similarly, even if I teach you the best study strategies in the world, if we're studying crap in the first place, we'll get nowhere.

Most students are overwhelmed by the huge amount of material presented in medical school. Some describe the experience as "trying to drink out of a fire hose." It's true, you're going to be presented with and asked to have a command of FAR more material than you could possibly become masterful of in such a short amount of time. This is a set-up for failure, stress, and disappointment.
Instead, it's far more useful to accept that there is no way you'll get it ALL done, but that you could find a way to master SOME material. Instead of doing what most students do and studying whatever they are told to study by the curriculum,

you can study the parts that are most important to you individually.

At the end of this section, you'll be able to have a much broader idea of the potential sources you could use to learn the science and practice of medicine, and after applying a variety of filters, you'll have a CUSTOMIZED, HIGH YIELD set of sources that you will use to learn medicine. These are your quality ingredients, and this is the core material you'll bring with you to the next section when we start to take a deeper look at the studying process itself.

Chapter 4: Creating Options: Discovering Potential Sources

Most students don't even think there is an option of what to study. What the syllabus says is what they do. I remember a political science course at my college where the syllabus had us reading an entire book a week! Really? There is NO WAY that would actually happen, and I would have been miserable trying to keep up with that but consistently failing. Medical school has been no different... For each hour of class, most of us are given lecture notes in PDF format, 30-100 PowerPoint slides, and "recommended reading" from several textbooks. Most students follow along with this schedule, and their lives become the nightmare that they heard about—working 16-hour days studying, and having no life for 4 years. This is NOT what we want to do.

Instead, we're going to look outside of the box at the various options for learning, here are some of the many options:

- Live Lectures
- Webcasted/Podcasted Lectures
- Lecture Notes
- Lecture PowerPoint Slides
- "Recommended Reading" Lists
- All of the above from a different medical school (i.e. if you have a friend who is at a school where the professor has great notes, and they can give you access to their school's material)
- Notes from other previous students
- Subject-Specific Books (i.e. Robbins Pathology or Abbas Immunology)
- Review Books (i.e. First Aid, Goljan Pathology)
- Medical Journals
- Audio Programs (i.e. Goljan, Recall)
- Online Video Reviews (i.e. Pathoma)
- Video Animations (i.e. molecular movies)

- Websites (i.e. UptoDate, Wikipedia, or other schools sites).
- Question Banks (i.e. USMLE World)

As you can see, this list could go on and on, but the point is that there are many more options for learning than you might notice at first glance.

And that's just it. These are only OPTIONS! This is the metaphorical sludge that is our starting point in the filter. It's sludge not because these are bad sources of information, but because it's too much information, and too broad. If we decide to learn all this sludge, we'll either have zero free time, or we will feel constantly behind, overwhelmed, stressed, and consequently will be very unproductive and unhappy—NOT what we want.

Process: Sourcing Sources

Before moving on, take a moment to look at the potential learning sources at your own school. Get a broad overview of how the curriculum is designed and how your school recommends you study and learn. Look at the lectures, labs, associated notes and lecture slides, "required" and recommended readings. Find out which classes or labs are mandatory and which aren't. Then start to brainstorm other potential options you've heard of (i.e. online question banks, review books, audio MP3 files, etc....) Later on, we will go into much more depth in finding out the best practices at your school, but for now, take 10-30 minutes to brainstorm and get an overview of what your learning options are. Write you answers down for reference. This is our starting point. This is our metaphorical mud that we're going to send through a series of filters, just like Dean Kamen's machine did, to arrive at a purified product.

Customized High Yield
Information

As you can see from this image, starting with this large amount of potential learning options, we're going to trim and refine them, using a variety of "filters" to arrive at a very high quality finished product—a customized, EXTREMELEY high yield, and SMALL amount of information, which will be our starting point for studying.

While in the image, it appears as if the filters are in blocks, one after the other, in reality, all three filters will be working together simultaneously to bring you the results you want.

Chapter 5: Filtering Through Your Personal Goals

Hopefully you've completed the processes from section 1 before arriving here. If not, go back and do that now. It's integral to know your own unique goals for medical school and your overall life in medical school before knowing which learning sources will be best for you. For example, if your goals were like me to have a lot of free time, master the core medical knowledge, and have the freedom to do any specialty, you might be best off to select learning sources that are portable (i.e. not lecture), and less detailed (i.e. review books instead of lecture notes). On the other hand, if your goals are to go into research, you might want to focus on choosing sources that go into much greater depth in your own field of interest (i.e. lectures, labs, suggested readings from professors), and review only the minimal information on the subjects you're less interested in (i.e. review books).

Remember to think outside the box as you do this. For example, if one of your goals is to develop a strong community of friends at your medical school, you might think that the best way to do this would be from going to lecture. This may be true, but another way of doing this that might work even better is to create more free time so that you can organize and attend more out-of-school social outings with your chosen friends.

Process: Filtering Through Your Personal Goals

Take out your sheet of goals from section 1 and compare it to the sheet of potential learning options you just made. Take 5-15 minutes to reflect on which potential learning sources might fit the best with your goals for med school and your life outside of school. For now, just circle or highlight those learning sources, keep your ideas fresh in your mind while you move on to the next filter.

40

Chapter 6: Filtering Through the Best Practices

For years I wanted to join the Peace Corps—what a wonderful way to give back, to learn a new culture and language, and to connect with the world. I even applied, and was accepted—TWICE! What held me back from going? I didn't want to re-invent the wheel. In the Peace Corps, you show up in a different country, are assigned to a community in need, and for the most part you are expected to figure out how to help them. I was smart enough to know that there had been people working on solving problems in the developing world for years, and it's very unlikely that I was going to just show up and figure out a better way. I didn't want to make the same mistakes made by everyone before me. Instead, I wanted to work with the true innovators in the NGO (Non Governmental Institution) world, the Steve Jobs', the Gandhi's, the Meg Whitman's of public health work—the people who found innovative solutions to create powerful lasting social change.

And that's exactly what I ended up doing instead. Following the advice of a family friend, I contacted senior non-profit consultants (who help train nonprofit organizations on how to be more effective in their work), and asked them who they thought the most innovative players were in grassroots public health. The organization with the most recommendations was a small NGO in India called the Jamkhed Comprehensive Rural Health Group. So I contacted them, asked if I could come out there to work for several months, and then off I went! In the process, I learned invaluable information about how to organize and inspire large groups of people to be caretakers of their own health while using limited resources (i.e. only 2 Medical Doctors caring for nearly 2 million people!)

The point of this story is that there are a huge amount of options for learning, and that these learning sources and learning experiences will vary greatly in quality. In the above example, had I done the Peace Corps, I would have been assigned to work with an organization, committed over 2 years of my life to the experience, and may or may not have learned what I was seeking. Instead, by finding the best practices for what I was looking for, I was able to pack in years worth of learning into several months!

You've already taken a moment to start thinking outside of the box about potential learning sources and reflecting on your personal goals. Now we're going to go deeper into that process to see which of these sources is the highest yield at your own school. Rather than go through a trial and error process, you want to learn from the mistakes of others, and start off where they left off on their own trial and error processes. This way we're STARTING at the TOP, where other top students have left off and building upon that. To do this, you'll first want to find the right people to ask and then ask them the right questions for what you want to know. At the end of this topic, you'll have a clear concise set of best practices for your own unique situation. Let's get started.

Step 1: Finding the Right People to Ask

If you ask 50 med students for their study tips, you'll get 50 different answers. Everyone is personally invested in his or her own system, but that doesn't mean that it works. You'll get answers from whomever you ask, so you want to be sure to talk to the students that are most likely to have valuable advice. These students will usually have 2 characteristics:

1. They got similar results to what you want to achieve

2. They recently finished whatever you're about to start

Let's take a look at these characteristics more deeply.

1. **They got similar results to what you want to achieve**: This will not be the same for everyone and will depend on your own unique goals. For example, if

you're like me, and have a triple goal of more free time and higher grades all while having more fun, you don't just want to talk to the people with the best grades, because it's likely that most of them spent the majority of their time studying to get those grades. Instead, I'd want to search for those that not only had top grades, but who also had a great life outside of school and seemed to be having fun. Similarly, if your goals are to be a researcher, you might want to seek out students who managed to publish several papers while simultaneously getting top grades. Your own unique goals will help guide you to find the right students to ask.

2. **They recently finished what you're about to start**. Usually, medical school works in various blocks or modules. Whether it's organ systems (GI, Hematology, Endocrine), or subject-based systems (Biochemistry, Pathology, Pharmacology), or large tests (i.e. Step 1), or third/fourth year clerkships, your experience will usually be divided in various 1 month to 4 month blocks. Therefore, the right students to ask for best practices will also be those who recently finished whatever block you are about to start, or whatever block you are curious about. Life lives in the details, and students who are far removed from whatever class your asking about will forget about the little details that make up the best advice. The sooner they finished, the fresher it will be on their minds.

Process: Finding the Right People to Ask

As you hold your own personal goals in mind, think about which students at your school best embody those goals. Don't limit yourself to people in your own class. Ask around and keep your eyes peeled for those people who have achieved similar results to what you want.

If top grades are one of your criteria, it can be awkward to ask other students their grades. In this case, do a little research—usually medical schools will have something like a "Dean's list for academic achievement" or "honor roll". It's likely that these students are the ones who did best academically. For other types of results, such as free time, you can usually figure this out by asking around or scanning your emails—are there some people that are leading most of the extracurricular activities, or are there some people that are known to be always traveling? Ask around and you'll find the answers you want.

Now, to the extent possible, find out which of those people have most recently finished the block you are about to enter Or, if your goal is to do well on Step I, find those top achievers, who did well on Step I, and also embodied your other goals. You won't need a lot of people because these are high quality people. One or two will suffice, and if you have a handful, you're golden. Once you find out who they are, get their contact info.

Step 2: Asking the Right Questions

These top students have a lot of great advice and best practices to offer, but often they don't know exactly what it is. If you ask them a general question, you'll likely get a general answer that won't be very useful. It's up to you to ask them the specific and unique questions that will draw out their precious knowledge and secrets that allowed them to get the results they did.

Here are some questions that I've found to be most helpful in drawing out best practices:

- What do you wish you knew before you started this System?
- If you could start this system/block/test prep phase again knowing what you know now, what would you do the same vs. differently?

- What curriculum resources were the highest yield? (You can go into a lot of detail here—which lecturers were best? Which notes were best? Which books? Which chapters in those books?)
- Which outside resources were the highest yield? Because curriculums are similar across the world, there are often high quality resources from other schools that are much more useful than your own school's materials, this could be audio tapes (i.e. Goljan), review books (i.e. First Aid), or even online videos/animations (i.e. molecularmovies.org).
- Which professors were the kindest or easiest to work with for doing research? Which made it easiest to publish a paper?

Ideally, try to poll several students to prevent bias from one individual's unique study habits.

I can't tell you how much this helped me and how many times it has helped. I've used this technique before starting every phase of med school, whether it be an organ system, a clerkship, or test-prep. I did this my first week of medical school and found out that one student had taken comprehensive notes, answering EACH learning objective of EACH class for the entire first 2 years of medical school... He distilled the notes, readings, and power points down to the specific learning points and cleanly typed out the answers, saved in a PDF that was accessible on his online website! I can't tell you how much time this saved. If I hadn't asked around, I would have never discovered that this resource existed!

Process: Ask Away!

Take a moment to see which questions are most relevant to what you want and send an email off to the students you selected from the process in Step 1. People are honored when you ask them for advice, and usually they are more than happy to give it. In my own experience, I've been blown away at how kind and helpful med students have been when I ask them for tips.

Chapter 7: Filtering Through Your School's System

By now you have a refined set of learning sources that are not only tested to be high yield at your school and in the block you're about to enter, but that also align with your own unique goals. You're off to a GREAT start. This next filter is not necessarily a sequential step after the last two, but more of complimentary step that is integral to know before moving forward—what are the rules of the game?

There are general rules that are common across medical schools, as well as specific rules that will be unique to your school. The more you know these systems and rules, the more empowered you'll be to make informed decisions about what you spend your time on.

Rule I: Every Medical School Has the Same Basic Rules

The Liaison Committee of Medical Education (LCME) is the organization that oversees medical schools in the US and Canada and determines whether or not they meet the requirements to give the degree of "M.D." to their graduates. Every several years, they do site visits of schools to make sure they're doing the necessary things to keep their eligibility. They look at everything from the organizational administration of medical schools, to the set-up of the curriculum, to the number of faculty and how they're governed, to the quality of the school library. They dictate the basic set-up of medical schools, and above and beyond this, schools have the freedom to design their school how they like it.

To practice medicine in the United States, students must pass several nationwide-exams designed and monitored by the National Board of Medical Examiners (NBME), a non-profit organization that creates and provides these exams. The

LCME decides whether students at a particular school are ELIGIBLE to take the USMLE (United States Medical Licensing Exam), and the NBME decides the basic curricular content that represents the core foundation of knowledge that a physician should have to practice medicine in the US. They offer curricular guidelines and learning objectives around which they base their test questions. Medical schools in turn use these guidelines and learning objectives to help shape their curriculum.

Rule II: Your Medical School Has Its Own System

Even though there are commonalities across all medical schools in the US and Canada, each school has the autonomy to do what they like within these basic rules. This is why some schools have a Problem Based Learning Approach (PBL) approach, while others have subject-based systems, and others have organ based systems. Some curriculums will be purely pass-fail, while others will have grades. Some will have mandatory attendance on all their classes while others might have only several mandatory classes. Knowing these rules will help you to make choices about how you want to spend your time.

Rule II, Part A: Tests

Tests themselves have their own systems of how they are designed by the curriculum committee, and knowing this information can be invaluable. For example, at my school, the system was that for every hour of lecture, a professor was allowed to write 2 questions that had to be based around the "learning objectives," which were clearly identified in the lecture notes. So, imagine that there was only one lecture on embryology, and that embryology was incredibly difficult to master (which it is), it would be much more useful for me to spend much less time on embryology and instead focus on the course material that had more devoted question and was easier to learn. Other schools may have a general pool of test questions that are re-used every several years. In this case, it might be most valuable to find old tests and focus studying around those questions.

Rule II, Part B: Attendance

Medical schools vary widely on how they set up lectures and whether or not they are webcasted or whether attendance is mandatory. Some of the guiding learning objectives, set by the LCME require you to be physically present (i.e. have so many hours working with patients, dissecting in anatomy lab, learning about professionalism and ethics), while others have optional attendance (i.e. lectures).

For some of these experiences, it really is valuable to be there in person. For example, it is incredibly difficult to learn anatomy well without touching a human body. Furthermore, many of the more humanities-oriented classes such as professionalism and ethics are much better taught in a seminar-style course with plenty of time for discussion. For most course content (i.e. lectures), classroom attendance is usually not mandatory, but demonstrated competence of that course work (i.e. passing tests) is required. This means the vast majority of classes are often optional—so should you go?

To answer this, let's take a look at the system of lectures, how they are designed, and how they're taught. Most schools hire PhD professors to perform research and teaching medical students is side-job that is a requirement for them. Similarly, many MD professors are asked to give lectures as an additional requirement to their clinical duties. These professors are usually given a set of learning objectives by your school's curricular committee to cover and are asked to design lectures around these objectives.

As you might imagine, most professors are going to craft their lecture around the learning objectives AS WELL AS their own research interests and personal experience. Very few, if any, are going to focus on teaching the learning objectives in a way that helps YOU best understand them for the boards and your future practice.

Of course, there are exceptions. Some professors are truly passionate about teaching students and go out of their way to make their lectures and notes very high-yield as well as entertaining and inspiring. These are classes you definitely want to make it to.

Knowing this part of the educational SYSTEM, you have a bit more information to help you decide whether you want to go to class or not.

Process: Get to Know the System

Starting from scratch, you've taken a plethora of potential options of what to study and how to study and then filtered them according to your own unique goals and the best practices (what's actually worked well for successful students). Now you'll filter this information again to further refine your learning sources based on how the system of medical school is designed both nationally and at your individual school. Let's get started.

Find the answers to the following questions. If you're not sure whom to ask, start with senior students and staff in the student affairs office.
- How are grades calculated for your various system blocks and/or for your third year clerkship blocks?
- How are lectures designed/structured? (I.e. does the curriculum committee give professors learning objectives that they MUST cover, and then the prof has free reign?)

- How many test questions does each professor get per hour of lecture?
- Are test questions based only on learning objectives? Are test questions based only on the lecture notes, or is it necessary to read the associated textbook readings to find the answers to some questions?
- How is AOA status calculated?
- What parameters are used to calculate "Dean's List" or the Honor Roll?
- Which classes are mandatory? Have exceptions ever been made? If so, for what? What happens if you miss a mandatory class?

These are a good starter list of questions, and no doubt as you start asking, you'll come up with more specific questions that apply to your individual case. By the end of this investigation, your goal is to know the relevant parts of the SYSTEM as they apply to your unique goals.

Should You Skip Class?

After getting a bit of knowledge of the system, many students start to question the value of going to class, and whether or not it's high yield for them. Because of this, I'm going to spend a little time covering some of the pros and cons of going to class vs. webcasting vs. other options.

At first, most students are terrified about the prospect of not going to class—"I'm paying so much money for school, isn't it a waste if I don't go to class?" "I can't motivate myself without class." "I'll get so behind if I don't go to class."
I believe there is no right or wrong choice... It comes down to how you learn best, and whether the tool of going to class helps you along toward your goals. Like everything else in life, you have a choice, and I want to make sure your choice helps you get to where you want to be.

While some medical schools have switched to a Problem Based Learning (PBL) format, which is more interactive, the majority are still lecture-based. Also, because there is so much material to learn in med school, these classes are information-packed, and there is very little discussion or reflection. Aside from a question here or there, communication is mostly one way--from professor to students. Furthermore, quality can vary greatly among professors. Now, professors aside, lectures are also complicated because of the learning environment.

At my school, we were all in a huge classroom fitting 160 people. Most students would sit in the back, nearly everyone with laptops open, and observing the classroom from the back of the room, about ¾ of the laptop screens were filled with ESPN, Facebook, YouTube, GChat, and other non-class related sites. Students were on their phones texting, talking to the students sitting next to them, and often laughing at inside jokes.

I did the exact same thing when I went to class. I used to be one of those sitting at the back of the class with my best friends, reminiscing about the party last weekend, talking about the latest news, while trying to listen (passively) to the professor. I had a blast in class, tons of fun, and I felt like I was doing something productive by being there and "listening." But did I remember much after the 50 minutes was over? Nope. Even if the professor was great, the environment was so distracting that it was nearly useless. I spent a full 9 hours on school related activity, but probably got 30 minutes worth of focused work done—pathetic.

Other students can focus very well in class. They are often the ones sitting up front, always asking questions, talking to the teachers after class with more questions, and always taking notes.

You're going to have to be honest with yourself, experiment with going to class and studying on your own and see if class is honestly a high-yield source of information for you.

For myself, and many other top-achieving students, class couldn't come close to matching the pace of learning we could achieve on our own, so we rarely went.
Now I'm speaking solely of didactic lectures... We also had many labs (gross anatomy, microbiology, etc.). I did end up going to many, but not all of these, and found most of them to be very high yield.

For example, I did not go to the microbiology labs because it wasn't one of my goals to be a microbiologist, and I knew that later in my career, I wouldn't have much use for knowing how to grow cultures or read agar plates. I did want to know the science, and I wanted to see some of the plates, but I could do this by quickly reviewing the lab PowerPoint rather than driving to school and physically attending the lab.

For Gross Anatomy and Neuroanatomy on the other hand, I really wanted to be there. Looking at pictures doesn't come close to the real experience, and it is something that is integral to a solid medical education. In this case, I always went to lab, but rather than just showing up and passively learning like I initially did in lectures, I would prepare for the lab in depth at home several days before using the study systems I'll cover in section 3. This way, by the time I went to the lab, it was more of a review and a test. I knew most of the structures we were identifying and was able to connect the cognitive knowledge with the tactile knowledge I gained in the dissection. This made attending labs VERY high yield.

So, the bottom line is to know yourself. If you are a class-learner, it's best to turn that experience into something high yield. That might mean preparing before, so that class is more of a final review, solidifying the details in your mind. Or, it might mean, that you sit up front, away from distractions, and close down Facebook and ESPN while in class. Only you know what will make it high yield for you, but if it's not high yield, why waste your time?

If I Don't Go to Class, Should I Webcast?

Many medical schools offer webcasts or podcasts of their lectures, which students can view from nearly anywhere. Although you miss out on the classroom environment, this offers you the option to review lectures whenever you want and in whatever environment you want.

Furthermore, most programs allow you to speed up the lecture to 1.5x – 3x speed, depending on what you can handle. The benefits of this are obvious—you can cut down the amount of time you spend in "lecture" dramatically, and for many students, they are able to concentrate better at this faster speed, which often demands their full attention to follow.

But—if you don't find that the lecture material or professor is a good learning tool for your goals, it's still not helpful to webcast, because if something isn't worth doing in the first place, it isn't worth doing twice as fast!

If I Don't Go to Class, Should I Study From My Lecture Notes at All?

Most people think if they don't go to class, they'll be at home studying the class lecture notes. Even this is simply one CHOICE out of many. Just because your school gives you a curriculum and schedule of classes, it doesn't mean you have to follow it. Even this is a choice. So, what to do?

To answer this, let's look again at how classes get constructed in the first place. As I mentioned before, the AAMC and AMA (who sponsor the LCME) are national organizations that connect and oversee all medical education in the US and Canada. These authorities dictate the basic medical curriculum and learning objectives every graduating student should be competent in, and medical school curricular committees take these guidelines to craft their curriculum and advise professors on how to structure their lectures.

As I mentioned before, most professors will focus their extra time along their own unique areas of research. If you are also passionate about that research, this could be a huge plus for you, as having interest in the material will inevitably help you to learn it better. However, if you aren't super passionate about the slant of the lecture material, you may be spending precious time learning something that is neither relevant to your future practice as a physician, nor relevant to the exams that matter in your future.

So if you decide you don't really want to use your lectures at all, or only use them minimally, what could you do instead? Here are some ideas:

- **Cherry Pick Professors Across the World**: Because medical school curriculums are so similar across the world, and because nearly all of them have online curriculums and webcast lectures, you could theoretically learn pathology from a professor in

California, learn physiology from a professor in Ohio, and biochemistry from a professor in New York. Of course, this would require that you have a lot of friends in different med schools across the world that will share their notes and webcasts with you. However, even if you don't, there are some professors out there whose material is available online. One of the most famous rock star teachers is the pathology legend, Edward Goljan, who has audio lectures and PDF notes available online, as well as his own review books. Another famous teacher for third year students doing surgery is Pestaña, who has some great review questions available online. As you expand your options, you can choose the professors you want to learn from, whose way of teaching matches your own unique style and goals.

- **Learn from Review Books as a Primary Source**: This is what I ended up doing most of the time. I used a high quality review source for the USMLE Step 1 (First Aid at the time of this writing), and started by learning this inside and out. For example, if I were about to start a 6-week course on the Musculoskeletal System, I would start by learning the first aid chapter on the musculoskeletal system inside and out. Then I'd turn to what I thought was the 2nd highest quality source (Goljan Rapid Review at the time) and learn the corresponding musculoskeletal chapter from that source. After these, with my extra time, I'd skim the learning objectives of my courses to make sure I knew them, which I almost always did by this point. If I didn't know one, I would review only that single lecture to fill in my learning gaps.

Process: Test Assumptions

After learning about the system at your school and reading this section, think about what might be best for you regarding your attendance in lecture. Over the next several weeks experiment with different strategies.

1. See what it feels like to go to class and sit in the front. Make yourself ask at least 3 questions per class, even if it seems like you don't have any questions. If you are too shy to ask in class, go up to the professor after class to ask your questions.
2. Try skipping class and webcasting lectures at various speeds.
3. Try skipping class and webcasting and only reviewing lecture notes and PowerPoint slides.
4. Try abandoning your schools curriculum altogether (at first, maybe 1 week) and instead; use the time you would have been in class to study from outside sources such as First Aid or Goljan's Rapid Review.
5. Try preparing ahead of time for labs and using them as "practice tests" rather than learning sessions.

In the following sections we'll go into much greater detail about the learning and studying process itself. For now, just try different strategies out to get a basic feel for what potential learning sources might work best for you!

Chapter 8: The Italian Filter

Do you remember when we went over "Pareto's principle" in the "Foundation" part of the book? He was the Italian economist who noticed that 80% of the land in Italy was owned by only 20% of the population. He later noticed that in his household garden, 80% of his produce of peas came from only 20% of his plants. His work later came to be down as "Pareto's Principle," commonly known as the 80/20 rule, and has been applied for decades in many fields—from business to software, from mathematics to politics.

As you filter down your learning sources from hundreds of potential options to several high yield sources, keep Pareto's principle in mind. The basic question to ask yourself is which 20% of input gives you 80% of your desired result? For example:

1. Which 20% of learning sources give me 80% of my knowledge?
2. Which 20% of lecturers give me 80% of my understanding of a topic?
3. Which 20% of labs give me 80% of my knowledge
4. Which 20% of my potential study partners give me 80% of my desired result (i.e. effective learning and fun)
5. Which 20% of subjects are responsible for 80% of my grade?
6. Which 20% of a book (i.e. Goljan Rapid Review) covers 80% of my school's learning objectives?

Example: Applying the Italian Filter to Get Interviews for Residency

For example, let's say that one of your goals is to get into your top choice residence in your top choice location. After speaking with several residency directors, the majority base their decision to invite a candidate for an interview on these factors (in descending order of importance):

1. United States Medical Licensing Exam Step 1 Score
2. Year 3 Clerkship Scores (Honors > High Pass > Pass)
3. Relevant Research
4. Quality of Letters of Recommendation
5. Quality of Personal Statement
6. Other—Deans Letter, Extracurricular Activities and CV, Grades from years 1 and 2, scholarships, etc...

These may vary slightly depending on the specialty or system (i.e. third year grades may be more important than step 1 score), but most residency directors will agree this is the basic order of importance.

Of your entire pre-clinical curriculum, perhaps only 20% or less is focused on preparing for the USMLE Step I, yet these results give you 80% or more of your desired outcome (getting an interview at your top choice residency).

Knowing this system and applying the Italian Filter, it makes much more sense to spend your time reviewing for the USMLE Step 1, even during your first year.

Because the USMLE Step 1 covers the majority of information that your curriculum will be designed around anyway, it's likely that simply by studying for Step 1, you will have enough knowledge to pass your current block exam. It's true, you won't likely get the top grade on your exam, but now that you know the system, you realize that a top grade doesn't really matter in the long run... If you have average grades on you school-based block exams, but a top grade on the USMLE Step 1, you'll be in far better shape for getting interviews where you want than a similar student who aced the block exams in the pre-clinical years but got an average grade on the USMLE Step 1!

Process: Apply the Italian Filter

Using the questions listed above as a starting point, brainstorm how you might apply the Italian Filter to your specific goals.

If answers to the questions above pop into your head right away, great! If not, keep this principle in the back of your mind as you continue reading, and come back and re-visit them in a few months to see if any new answers emerge for you as you continually refine and improve your learning process.

Congratulations! You've finished a very important part of your study process that will serve you well—selecting the perfect ingredients for YOU. You've turned sludge into Evian.

Let's review what you've done.

> **Start:** You started with that metaphorical sludge of potential learning materials, the raw content that most med students don't think twice about and begin studying, only to get overwhelmed and stressed when they realize they're not learning fast enough, and can't possibly complete it all.

> **Filter 1: Your Goals.** You sifted through this huge amount of information through the filter of your own personal goal for what you want to learn in medical school and what you want from your life outside of school during these 4 years, and arrived at a refined group of learning sources that is customized toward your own unique goals.

> **Filter 2: Best Practices.** You then took these learning sources and filtered them again by keeping only the ones that fit with the best practices of the top-performing students at your own individual school.

> **Filter 3: The System.** You learned about the system of how medical school curriculums are designed in

general, as well as the system at your specific school. You also learned in greater detail about the some of the pros and cons of going to lectures or labs as well as some other options you could do instead. Using this knowledge, you further refined your learning sources to see which are not only High Yield and aligned with your goals, but also work well given the system and design of your school.

Filter 4: The Italian Filter. Just like Pareto, you sifted through your already refined list of learning sources to pick apart those that are the highest yield, keeping only the most effective 20% of sources. Final Product. Just like Dean Kamen's miraculous machine, you've turned a HUGE amount of potential learning material into a VERY SMALL amount of customized, high yield learning sources.

Your final product should meet these specifications:

- **Size**: Your final product should be a VERY SMALL amount of information. It should be so small that you should be thinking in the back of your mind—"I should really be studying more than this." Remember, you can always add more information later.

- **Quality**: Ask yourself, "If I knew this material inside and out, if I had it totally mastered, would it be enough for me to get the grade I want on the exam?" Your answer should be yes. You probably won't know this intuitively at first when you start doing this, but as you practice, it will come more easily.

This material is the crystal clear Evian water that you can bottle up and bring with you to the next section, where you'll learn the tools to master this information in record time.

Section III: Learning 2.0

The entire amount of information known by the entire human race in 0 A.D. was doubled by the time we got to 1500 A.D. This is known as the "doubling time" and back then, it was 1,500 years. The current "doubling time" of information is just 7 years--every 7 years, the amount of information known to the human race doubles!!! What's more is that the doubling rate is only getting smaller and smaller. It's nearly impossible to even imagine how much information will be available to us during our lifetimes in medicine.

Yet, despite the incredible gain in human knowledge, how much has really changed about the WAY we learn? The University of Bologna, established in 1088, is the oldest university still operating today. While the equipment in its labs, and the information being taught is vastly different than it was back in 1088, how much has a student's learning and studying experience really changed? Students still sit in lecture halls listening to professors and taking notes. They still read books. Yes, some schools have replaced lectures with webcasts, and handwritten notes are being replaced by computer-typed notes, but the basic format is still the same.

Is it possible that the learning experience can be re-invented, that we could take the exponentially increasing knowledge of the human mind and memory, and design a different learning system from that point? Indeed it is!

In this section, I'll begin by giving you a basic overview of the brain and how it's structured both on a gross level as well as on a microscopic level. I'll then go into some of the basic principles of how learning happens, how memories are encoded, and how you can apply some of these principles to how you study. Then we'll take another look at how the average medical student studies so you can see with greater clarity why this is far from ideal. Finally, I'll go into a very different learning system that works in accordance with how the brain is designed. I'll teach it to you in writing first, and then give you raw, detailed over-the-shoulder-style videos that show you exactly how to put this into practice.

When most students try to get better grades, they look for better learning sources (i.e. getting the newest edition of First Aid or subscribing to USMLE World), very rarely paying attention to the WAY they're learning the information in the first place. We often get locked into learning habits and superstitions we've had for a long time, some of which may be effective, others of which may be very inefficient.

By taking some time to zoom out and reflect both on how you've been learning as well as how the latest neuroscience says the brain works, you'll be doing yourself a huge favor. You'll be able to tailor your study techniques to the way the brain learns, and thereby achieve exponentially more efficient results.

This section is the CRUX of the book. By the end of it, you'll not only have a clear idea of practical information about how the brain works when it comes to learning, but you'll also have a very clear picture of how to apply these techniques towards your studies. You will know a study SYSTEM that you can use for all your subjects, and through the included videos, you'll know exactly how to get started with your first study session.

Chapter 9: Designing a Learning System with the Brain in Mind

The brain is easily the most complex organ in the human body, and the most advanced computer that exists in the world. A 3-pound, gelatinous sphere, filled with glia and neurons that burn glucose like a supercharged hummer burns gas. It makes up about 1% of our body mass, but burns 20% of our ATP, that means it uses 1,400% more energy pound per pound!

Our brains contain an average of 100 BILLION neurons. Each of these neurons AVERAGES 10,000 connections to other neurons, and sends electrical-chemical signals that represent either an on/go signal or an off/stop signal at any given moment. This means we have over 100 TRILLION neuronal connections in our brains. The number of POSSIBLE on/off neuronal firing patterns in one brain is $10 \times 10^{1,000,000}$. That is more than the number of atoms in the entire known universe!

A storm of electrical impulses is shooting through these connections at a speed of over 250 miles per hour, resulting in our unconscious and conscious experience of life. And the inter-connections between neurons are constantly changing based on their firing patterns (even as you read this, your neural networks are shifting). Needless to say, the brain is incredible.

The General Structure of the Brain

Many of you may know neuroanatomy already in great detail; however if you are pre-med or just starting medical school, I'll do a quick review that will cover enough for you to understand this section. I find the easiest way to explain the brain is by using your fist as a model. To make this model, open your hand, fold in your thumb, and then close your fingers into a fist. Your wrist represents your spinal cord, which takes information to and from most of the rest of your body. Your palm represents your brain stem which helps control such

basic unconscious things as heart rate, breathing, and
wakefulness. Your thumb (imagine a thumb coming in from
the other side too so that it's symmetrical) represents the
limbic system, which works together with your brainstem to
regulate and control our emotions, our basic drives, and much
of our memory. The back of your hands and fingers represent
the neocortex, our uniquely human invention, composed of an
approximately 2.6 square foot sheet of brain matter folded in
on itself to fit within our skulls.

As you might imagine, different parts of the brain are
responsible for different things. In fact, each of our five senses
is mapped on a different part of the brain. Our vision is
represented in the back of our brain, sound goes to the sides of
our brains, smell and taste are processed in two different
regions in the lower front part of our brains, and touch is
represented in a horizontal line (from ear to ear) over the tops
of our brains. Our emotions are mapped in the central part of
our brain (your thumbs), and information from our internal
organs and the rest of the world comes in through the spinal
cord and cranial nerves (located in the brainstem).

An Inside Look at a Neuron

Within this 3-pound mass lie nearly 100 BILLION neurons.
Each neuron is a rather large cell, resembling something like a
tree. They communicate with each other through their roots,
and trunks, called dendrites and axons, respectively.

All of the information in our outside world (smells, tastes,
physical sensations, pictures, and sounds) is converted into
electrical and chemical symbols by specialized sensory sells
and then sent to thousands of neurons in the brain to generate
an electrical network that encodes our experience of reality.

Furthermore, new research in neuroscience suggests the
existence of mirror neurons, which mirror the same firing
patterns of people around us. This suggests that we are also
getting information from OTHER PEOPLE'S nervous systems
that contribute to our internal representation of the world.

Imagine something akin to a three-dimensional spider web. These networks are not set in stone, but constantly changing and morphing themselves, based on when and where they are receiving electrochemical energy. Our internal states (such as our subjective emotional state and where we place our attention) also control and direct this flow of energy and information within our brains.

The Framework for a Memory: Everything is Connected

Take about 30 seconds to think about what you had for dinner last night. Contemplate the meal in detail for the full 30 seconds before reading on.

What came to mind? Just the foods on the plate? Or did you also see the plate, and the whole room you ate in? Did you also remember the conversation you had at dinner? The smell and taste of the food? The pain from accidentally biting your tongue? The excitement of the party you went to after eating?

The point of this little exercise is to show you that our experiences and our memories are coded in networks.... you just don't' remember one single aspect of an experience, but when you attempt to remember any one part of the memory, the whole network of experience comes up in your mind.

Let's imagine a "simple" example of a single moment in class. As you watch the professor, electromagnetic radiation in the form of light is captured and transformed into chemical signals in your retina, then transferred into electrical signals that eventually end up in the back of your brain in the visual cortex. The vibrations of the teacher's voice are conducted through the air in sound waves until they hit your tympanic membrane that moves tiny bones in your middle ear which in turn create vibrations in your cochlea, a fluid filled sac in your inner ear that is lined with small hair-like structures that detect the movement of the fluid and convert it into electrochemical signals that travel to your brainstem and eventually end up within the auditory cortex in your temporal lobes. The pressure from that uncomfortable plastic chair you're sitting on is detected by sense organs in your skin and then transferred to electrochemical signals that end up in the sensory cortex on the top of your brain. The flavors of the Orange Mocha Frappuccino you're drinking travel through three different cranial nerves and are mapped to the bottom of your brain. And that BO smell of the guy behind you who just came from the gym is also converted into electrical signals and mapped onto your olfactory cortex, also at the lower front part of your brain.   Finally, all the information above can trigger and activate old emotional memories from the limbic system in the core of your brain. Because all these networks are activated at the same time, these neurons become connected with each other in a unique electrical network that represents your experience in that moment. This is your initial framework for a memory from that class.

These networks are forming and dissolving all the time. Obviously, most of us don't remember every single thing that's ever happened to us. Even though 100 billion neurons is a lot of processing power, our brain's capacity is still limited. The initial memory network is very fragile. I like to think of it as a line drawn in the sand along the beach. After two or three waves pass by, it's gone.
To keep our memories and their associated neural networks alive longer, we need to strengthen them. But how?

Chapter 10: How to Supercharge Your Memory

What follows are the basic principles to encode rich memories and strengthen them so they last for a long time. These principles are here to get you thinking about ideas of how memory works and how to learn better. Don't worry too much now about putting them all into practice. At the end of this section, I'll teach you a learning system that puts them all into practice in great depth. For now, just read, think, and enjoy.

Make it Complex From the Beginning

What's fascinating is that neuroscience has shown us that this initial network of neurons that you used to form the first memory, is the VERY SAME network you use to store a permanent memory! Also, we know that each time you activate one part of the memory network; the entire network is activated and strengthened.

So, when you make a memory, you want to make it as multi-sensory, and as interconnected as possible. In practical terms, this means having diagrams as well as text (which are processed in different parts of the brain), have a stimulating audio experience (whether that's listening to an interesting lecturer, or music), have a tangible physical experience (such as writing something on a pen and paper or typing), be sipping on a tasty drink, and maybe be sitting outside in a fragrant flower garden. Of course there are many ways to make the initial network rich and inter-connected with many senses to activate our entire brain, but you get the idea. We'll go into more detail later.

Build upon Existing Networks

Another fascinating discovery from Neuroscience research is that when we add new associations to pre-existing memory networks, not only is the new memory activated and strengthened, but so is the ENTIRE memory network it's associated with! For example, if you wanted to build a 3-foot spider web, it's much easier to add an inch onto a web that is already 2 feet 11 inches rather than start from scratch. Using this same metaphor, imagine that if you wanted to make a 3-foot web stronger, you would only need to add an inch to one part of the web, and it would make the entire web thicker and stronger! Knowing this, the easiest way to make a memory network more complex is to connect it to an already pre-existing network. There are two ways to use this principle while learning—Priming, and Connecting the Dots.

Priming

Priming simply means that before you begin a new subject, you get a brief overview of the big picture of the subject, and begin to connect it to what you already know.

Ask yourself these questions:
- What do you already know about this subject?
- What have you learned before?
- What are the most important principles and concepts of this subject?

For example, suppose you are about to start the microbiology system. You might start studying by doing a brief overview of the entire subject, such as skimming the corresponding chapter in First Aid, not for memorization, but just so that you have a minimal familiarity with the terms and the types of things you'll be learning the upcoming month.

Skimming something like first aid is especially helpful not only because it helps you prime, but also because it will help you be aware of the most important (and testable) parts of the subject, so that you'll be able to quickly differentiate later in the month which things are worth spending the extra time to know well vs. which things are less important.

By priming your brain in this way, you're weaving a HUGE but thin web that covers the entire subject you'll be doing. Each time you learn something new, or learn something more in depth on this subject, the entire memory network will strengthen.

Connecting The Dots

This means that you're actively connecting the subject with other parts of your life related to it. In our microbiology example, it means you're remembering when you had strep throat and what that felt like and what happened to your body, or when you watched the movie "Outbreak" and learned about the Ebola virus, or when you saw the news in Haiti about the Cholera outbreak after the earthquake.

Make it personal too--think about some questions you have already on the topic. For example, what are you curious about in microbiology? Are you going on a trip to Panama and want to know if you need malaria prophylaxis? Which one? Why that one? How does it work? Will you need the yellow fever vaccine? How will you know if you need to take Cipro for that diarrhea you're having?

By doing this, you're connecting the memory network you created by priming to hundreds of other pre-existing networks in your brain that are all related to microbiology. These networks are incredibly rich, because they're connected to emotions, multiple senses, and different times in your life.

By creating a rich initial network (priming) and connecting it to existing networks of memories (connecting the dots), you're giving yourself a huge head start, and once you start taking in new information, you'll be getting much more bang for your buck.

Keep it Fresh

Think about the last time you were in a car driving from your home to a new place. It's likely that once you glanced at the first few directions from your home, you went on autopilot and could easily listen to music or talk to a friend on your Bluetooth headset. However, what happened once you exited the freeway and entered new territory. You probably couldn't talk on the phone anymore, and you probably needed all of your attention on the road. This is because your brain comes alive when presented with new situations. Studies show that when data is presented in a new way or in a new environment, you learn more effectively. I'll talk about how to put this into practice in the next section.

Spaced Repetition

Neuroscience tells us that the mechanism that strengthens neural networks when they're activated is spaced repetition. When a specific connection between two neurons is activated repeatedly in spaced intervals, a message is sent to the nucleus of those cells to activate DNA that will make new proteins to strengthen that particular connection. The result is that more information can pass through that channel, and, thus the information can travel faster.

The German psychologist, Hermann Ebbinghaus dedicated his life to understanding human memory. Through his research, he developed what he called the "leaning curve" and the "forgetting curve;" the latter showed that without repetition, humans forget 90% of the information they learn after 30 days. With spaced repetition however, the amount one is able to remember increases exponentially.

So, the more you can repeatedly activate a network, the stronger the network becomes and the more easily you'll be able to remember it. Knowing this, the way to learn is through seeing the material again and again, and ACTIVELY remembering it over and over spaced out throughout time.

Passive repetition would be something like re-reading a chapter in a book, but ACTIVE repetition would be more like a flashcard--asking yourself a question and forcing yourself to think about and come up with an answer before flipping the card over to see if you're right. The more you ACTIVLEY recall memory networks, the more permanent the memory network becomes.

Imagine how ideal this concept is in a medical setting. If you can develop strong memory networks when you initially learn the material in your first two years, they will be enriched and re-activated in your clinical years as you see the same pathology and treatment, but in a different setting and with new information. In my own clinical years, I was amazed at how much of the basic science just popped into my head without effort when I activated an old strong network I had developed in my pre-clinical years.

Once you realize these principles, you realize the futility of cramming. In cramming, you're loading up a rich initial network with maybe a few instances for short spaced repetition, which keeps the network alive long enough to perform on the test, but as you might imagine, without the longer-term spaced repetition, it is not strong enough to survive for long, and after a few months is nearly gone, forcing you to re-learn it for your end of year finals and for the boards. Not a very efficient use of your time.

The Fertilizer Trinity: Attention, Emotion, and Exercise

In addition to these basic principles for forming and enhancing memories, there are a few very high yield tricks that act like Miracle Grow for baby memory networks. Let's go over each of them.

Attention

Multitasking is a myth. The brain can only pay conscious attention to a single thing at a time. When people think they are multitasking, what they are actually doing is rapidly switching between single points of attention so that it SEEMS like they're paying attention to many things at the same time. This concept has been shown repeatedly in fMRI studies.

Think of your attention like a fertilizer hose--wherever you point that house, neural networks are going to grow bigger and stronger, because all of your brain's resources are heavily allocated to whatever you are focused on. In fact, through our focused attention, we can actually re-wire the networks in our brain.

UCLA psychiatrist and neuroscientist Jeffrey Schwartz coined the term "Self-Directed Neuroplasticity" and has used this principle to successfully treat Obsessive Compulsive Disorder without medications. By intentionally focusing and re-focusing their mental energy (thoughts) towards what they want rather than their destructive obsessions, patients physically change the microanatomy of their brains to eliminate the patterns causing their disease. In this way, their "sick networks" get weaker and their "healthy networks" get stronger.

We can apply this same principle as students to strengthen and empower our memory networks by working in short but highly focused chunks of time. It's very difficult to sustain a high level of attention and mental concentration, but the pay-off is exponentially greater than studying for long periods with only partial focus. For example, 90 minutes of 100% focus on your material can give you better results than 3-4 hours of "studying" where you are frequently interrupted and only partially attentive to what you're studying. When we can focus close to 100% of our attention on what we're studying, the short and long-term learning payoff is huge. While doing this, we can still be taking in multi-sensory experiences (sights, sounds, smells, etc....) that are actually helpful, but our single point of ATTENTION is focused on what we're studying, not elsewhere--fertilizing the exact memory network we want to. In the next section, we'll go more into the optimal study environment and practical tips of how to apply this principle.

Additionally, the more often we keep our ATTENTION on and remember our overall goals for medical school and life (which we defined in section I), the stronger that network will be in in our minds, and the more likely we will be to remember our vision and to continue to move toward it. Like I mentioned section I, it's useful to write down your goals and keep them in a visible place to remember them (and thus recharge their associated neural networks) over and over.

Emotion

There are few neural fertilizers that can strengthen a memory more than strong emotion. Think back to your earliest memories in childhood right now. It's likely that the ones you remember were linked to a strong emotion—the fear of being left alone in your crib in the dark, or the joy of petting a dog for the first time.

Emotions engage our primitive mammalian brain structures to enrich and strengthen our pre-existing memory networks.

The emotion doesn't have to be super intense to work as a neural fertilizer. Take the initial example of a lecture where we went over all the sensory information coming into you. Now let's add emotion. Let's say that while you're in class, it also happens to be Friday, and you're feeling excited and happy about the weekend to come. In this case, your limbic system fires up and joins the party, converting your emotion into electrical signals from the center of your brain and plugging into the entire network from your senses, helping the entire memory network of what you're learning to grow stronger.

Even if it's Monday, you can still put this to work while you learn and study. It's true that any emotion works, so if you're a bit masochistic, you could try to be angry or sad while studying. However, I would hope that most of us would choose to be joyful. Putting joy and studying in the same sentence may seem like an oxymoron to you right now, but for now just pretend that it might be possible, and ask yourself—how could I actually have fun studying? Take a moment to reflect on what comes to mind without editing it. Think outside of the box here...

Some ideas that I used are:
- Study in a lively fun coffee shop
- Invite friends to study "with me" (we'll talk more about group studying later, but here I mean studying independently but sitting at the same table, maybe taking breaks together)
- Listen to some new music while studying
- Invite your crush from class to study together, and then grab dinner after

- Study (by listening to lectures and audio reviews) while snowboarding, or running, or while climbing an iced-over volcano in Chile using ice picks (yes, I actually did that). Here, the single point of attention is on the lecture material you are listening to, and you are on "cruise control" in the activity you are doing (similar to driving while listening to the news on NPR).

The more you think outside of the box here, the more you see that the options are limitless...It is more than possible to have fun while studying, and by doing so, not only does the time pass more enjoyably, but it also helps you remember what you're studying MUCH better.

Exercise

As famous neuroscientist John Medina writes about in his book[4], we were designed to learn while exercising. He even goes so far as to recommend that instead of desks in classrooms, we have treadmills where students learn while walking fast or doing a slow jog.

The latest "hardware upgrade" to our anatomical brains happened with the evolution of Homo Sapien from Homo Erectus about 200,000 years ago! This was during a time when a "typical day" involved moving from cave to cave, hunting animals, gathering berries, and learning outside in nature. Supposedly the average caveman walked about 12 miles a day! Not surprisingly, our brains tend to learn best while we're active.

Over and over again, studies show that people who live an active lifestyle perform better on every possible test of cognition. Regular aerobic exercise is still thought of

---

[4] Medina, J. (2008). Brain rules: 12 principles for surviving and thriving at work, home, and school. Seattle, WA: Pear Press.

the most powerful tool to prevent Alzheimer's dementia, and has even been shown to be EQUALLY effective[5] in treating mild depression as medications like Zoloft!

Not only does exercise have a positive long-term cumulative effect, but it also helps us form and enrich memory networks in the moment. Aerobic exercise causes the release of two important chemicals in the brain. The first is a peptide called Brain Derived Neurotrophic Factor (BDNF). This is like fertilizer for your brain cells, helping them to grow faster, stronger, and bigger connections wherever BDNF is present. Exercise has been shown in many studies to increase BDNF in the brain's memory center—the hippocampus.

Furthermore, aerobic exercise triggers blood vessels to release Nitric Oxide, a potent vasodilator that allows substantially more oxygen and glucose to reach our neurons. The result is akin to adding NOS to a car engine—our brains get Turbocharged. What's more, these benefits were shown with JUST 20 minutes of aerobic exercise three times a week, and the results were further improved if strength training was added!

You can apply this not only by exercising regularly, but also by learning while exercising. Through audio information, such as the famous Goljan lectures or lecture podcasts, you can get great results by listening to them while you exercise. As you get used to this form of learning, you'll likely notice that your ability to concentrate is greatly improved, you learn very well, and have fun doing it. So give it a try!

---

[5] Babyak M. Exercise treatment for major depression: maintenance of therapeutic benefit at 10 months. Psychosom Med 2000 Sep-Oct; 62(5): 633-8.

Putting it All Together

Now that you understand the basics of how memories are formed and retained, lets turn our attention to designing an ideal system to assist our brains in learning the way they were made to learn. To review, we are looking for a learning system that is:

- **Complex:** Involving as many senses as possible (visual text and diagrams, audio, smells, tastes, physical touch)

- **Built Upon Existing Networks:** i.e. allows you to easily personalize and customize information to connect it to your pre-existing memory networks.

- **Incorporates Spaced Repetition:** Uses ACTIVE learning and spaced repetition to encode information into your long-term memory

- **Focused:** Allows you to focus with a high level of attention for short bursts.

- **Fun:** Allows you to experience a sense of joy (or any positive emotion) while studying.

- **Aerobic:** Allows you to either have enough free time so that you have time to exercise and/or allows you to learn WHILE exercising.

- **Efficient:** In addition, to make this efficient for us, we want this system to be very easy and FAST to use.

Chapter 11: Why Traditional Study Strategies Don't Work

Before jumping into learning a way of learning that would meet those requirements, let's take another look at the way most medical students study, and what's why it doesn't work so well.

Next time you're in lecture, take a look around and see what people are doing. Ask a few of your friends how they are studying and learning the material. Most often, people will be doing the same things they've been doing since they started school—Going to class, reading, highlighting nearly the entire book, taking notes, and then studying their notes.

This basic system CAN work, and I know many very successful students who used a similar system to study, however, they spent nearly their ENTIRE DAY doing this, had very little free time, and were almost always at a high-stress level. Let's look at why this is less than ideal.

- **Not Complex:** While lectures may involve diagrams and pictures, when most students study and read and make notes, they are using text alone. After all, it takes lot of time to re-draw a diagram or include a picture in with your notes.

- **Their Networks, Not Yours:** This way of learning is based on your professors learning networks. They teach the material in a way that is connected to THEIR own previous experiences and interests, which may or may not be similar to yours. Furthermore, this way of studying is not personalized. Most students are uniquely stronger in some parts of the material, and weaker in others. In this system, equal weight is given to each lecture regardless of how strong you are in the material. Even if you make personalized notes, you'll find that as the weeks pass, you'll be stronger in some parts of those notes, and weaker in other parts. In the old way, there is no easy and fast way to cherry-pick the parts you are weakest in and focus specifically on improving those.

- **Not Designed around Spaced Repetition:** Usually, each lecture is it's own content, and you see it once, maybe study it after class, and then maybe review it the week before the test. Also, most students will fall behind in studying and instead cram before a test— using a lot of time and energy to keep the information in their short-term memory only to lose it again a few days after the test.

- **No Focused Bursts of Attention:** Unfortunately, no one is able to concentrate at near 100% attention for very long; however the old way of learning requires very long hours—sometimes up to 6-8 hours of lecture and lab a day, followed by studying and reviewing the class material. This forces students to spread out their focus and attention very thinly, never getting the full beneficial effects that total focus can bring.

- **No Time for Exercise:** I'm assuming that your lecture halls don't have treadmills instead of seats— although it'd be cool if they did. Also, most students are often so busy with learning that the free time for daily exercise simply doesn't exist, and you lose out on the powerful fertilizer effects of exercise.

- **Not Necessarily Joyful:** This is pretty subjective, and I really hope that most of you have the ability to feel totally joyful and excited while pulling long hours in school, but if you're like me, to sustain joy, you need free time and freedom to do what you want, including relationships and hobbies outside of school. When I have the time to sleep, eat well, exercise, and pursue my outside interests, I'm able to study with joy, bringing in all the beneficial brain fertilizer effects.

In addition to the basic brain principles we covered, the traditional way of studying is also off in several other important ways.

- **Focus on Passive Learning:** This means your professor or curriculum committee is telling you WHAT to study (the curriculum), and HOW and WHEN to study (by going to class using the schedule they give you). The information is typically presented in lecture format and all that is required is you sitting in lecture and "soaking up" the information. True active learning would be not only re-forming the material in your own words, but also being able to re-produce the material from a question, and even be able to teach others the material (notice that tests are presented in such an active question-answer format). When you use a mostly passive-learning process to prepare for an active-recall exam, you will not perform your best.

- **Builds False Confidence:** This system of learning can take many, MANY hours, making you THINK you're really doing a lot of learning. After all you're spending nearly your whole day doing it! After spending a 12-hour day studying material by attending lecture, reading, and taking notes, it's easy to convince yourself that you have a good command of the information. But did you ever try to take a practice quiz the following day? How did you do? Likely not great. That's because all that was formed in that 12 hours of lecture was a weak initial memory network. The information was never strengthened and sealed into long-term memory. It's easy to convince ourselves that we know something, because as we read a chapter, we are forming an initial memory network, but if we just read and take notes, we stop there, never sealing the information network into our long-term memory.

- **Time-Intensive:** As you can imagine, it can take a long time to pre-read for lectures, attend them and take notes, do the suggested readings while taking notes, consolidate your notes, and then review your notes and re-consolidate. Indeed, this will take your entire day, and you still will feel rushed and short of time.

Hopefully by now you've had some time to reflect on why the normal way of studying and learning is less than ideal. I don't necessarily think it's anyone's fault. It's just that people often spend their time focusing on making better material than on improving the system of how people learn that material.

Chapter 12: A Learning System Designed for Our Brain

After learning more about the brain, talking to hundreds of students about best practices, experimenting myself, and teaching others, I've arrived at a system of learning that not only works well, but also works in line with how our brains are designed to learn.

First, I'll walk you through how I arrived at this system, and then I'll teach it to you in detail... Buckle your seat belts!

The Flash Card

Dr. Paul Farmer, founder of Partners in Health, Harvard Medical School Professor, and a tireless human rights activist is one of my lifelong heroes. When I first heard about him through the book, Mountains Beyond Mountains, I was not only impressed by the medical humanitarian work he does, but also with how he led his life while going through medical school at Harvard. Farmer spent nearly all of his time in "medical school" living in Haiti and running a free clinic. He made special arrangements to fly back for exams, and graduated near the top of his class. He treated medical school like a part-time job while simultaneously building one of the worlds most innovative and successful public health non-profit organizations.

While most students worried about simply surviving the rigors of medical school, Farmer trusted that he would find a way to learn while following his deep passion to be a doctor to the world's poor. His example was like a bright torch to me in a cave of darkness, I had worried that life in medical school would kill my soul, robbing me of opportunities to explore other interests. He showed me that we are limited only by our imaginations.

So how did he pull this off? He was obviously smart and driven by a deep passion for service. But there must have been more to it. I combed his biography, looking for his study secrets. And then I found it: flashcards. He made extensive flashcards for every subject and his girlfriend would quiz him whenever there was a free moment -- whether it was an 8 hour bumpy bus ride surrounded by chickens and goats, on a hike to visit a sick patient living in the hills of Haiti, or in between seeing patients at the rural hospital he built. Could it really be that simple?

I decided to give it a try. My first attempt at making flashcards was in Gross Anatomy. I took 4x6 inch index cards and tore them in half, grabbed my favorite ballpoint pen and went to work. I listed names of bones, nerves, vessels on one side, and their function on the other side. This was great! I made and reviewed the cards before our dissections, and by the time we got started, I was thrilled to see how much I remembered. In our dissections, the information network I had created with my flashcards was re-activated and enriched with multi-sensory information from the cadaver itself. When we revealed a new muscle with our scalpel, I would automatically hear the name of the muscle in my mind and simultaneously link the name to its function, blood supply, and nerve supply. It was effortless!

Within a few weeks, I had hundreds of flashcards, bunched together with rubber bands. As I reviewed them, I'd set them in different piles according to how well I knew them. One pile had cards I knew on the first try; another had those I could get on the 2nd try. Then there were those that took several rounds to commit to memory. With each study round, the card decks got smaller and smaller, and when test day rolled around, I had a relatively small amount of material to review, and it was customized to my own unique weak points in the material.

Even though flashcards greatly improved my ability to learn and memorize the massive volume of information coming at me in medical school, there were still some problems. First, they took forever to make. I was making hundreds of cards a week, and I couldn't write fast enough to get all the material down. Calluses began to grow in places I've never seen them before on my hands, and on some days, my hands would just quit working out of sheer exhaustion. Then there were subjects such as biochemistry and physiology that lent themselves more to diagrams than words, and it would take a while to hand draw these diagrams on each card. The huge amount of time spent on making the cards was not very high yield, and most of it was mindless cutting, writing, drawing, rubber banding, and sorting.

Finally, there was the sheer volume of cards. The card decks became so large that I put them in large zip-lock bags arranged by subject, and I'd often need a separate bag to carry them with me to the library. There were times when I wanted to review a certain subject, and it began to take me longer and longer just to find the cards I wanted to review. As the decks of cards began to grow larger and larger, it became clear to me that despite it's value in building strong long-term memories and mastery of a subject, this system was unsustainable as a primary learning device, at least the way I was using it.

Most students come to this same conclusion and either give up on using flashcards, or use them as an adjunct learning tool, making a very small amount of cards to review before tests. But, what would learning be like if there was a way to capture all the value of the flashcard format without the problems of a paper-based system?

The Game Changer: The Electronic Flashcard

Just like it's done with nearly every field of life, technology comes to the rescue to make things faster, easier, and just plain better. The same was true with flashcards. Late in my first year of medical school, my cousin, a Macintosh computer genius who knew of my study habits, sent me an e-mail that had a link to a computer software program designed to make electronic flashcards. I didn't pay too much attention at first, but this turned out to be the perfect solution and one of the primary tools behind my academic success.

It took me nearly a year before I took full advantage of this tool. At first, I used it to make flashcards similar to what I had made on paper – I merely typed the information on the front and back. This step alone solved several issues. I type faster than I write, so I made cards faster. They also were easier to carry and sort because they were all digital and on my computer. And they were SEARCHABLE! That means that if I felt weak on one particular concept, I could search my flashcard database and all the information I had on that concept would pop up in seconds! Before, this would have taken hours of combing through hundreds of flashcards. But, typing the information onto the card was still time consuming and not the most efficient use of my time.

"Flashing"--The New Way to Read

Another light bulb went off when I realized that most of our material was becoming digitized. When I began medical school, schools had just begun to webcast lectures online. Now, our entire syllabus is online, our notes are in Adobe PDF format, and the lecture slides themselves are listed on the website as downloadable PowerPoint files. What's more, textbook publishers have Kindle and other e-book editions, and there are searchable internet-based versions of textbooks. Medicine is moving online, and this shift has many implications for how the modern student can study.

Now, instead of typing material onto a flashcard, I could further simplify the process by copying and pasting large chunks of text into cards. I could also attach diagrams and pictures onto the cards themselves to quiz myself not only on written data, but also with pictures of the body on a micro and macro level. Eventually, even copying and pasting became too slow, and I would use screenshots to "take pictures" of books or lecture notes, and use this information on my cards.

This process became so fast and efficient, that I eliminated "reading" altogether. Most students use flash cards as an add-on to their traditional reading/notes way of studying. But if flashcards are a superior way to learn, why not use them as the core comprehensive tool?

Why read whole chapters when you can learn the material from the first time in bite-sized chunks? This is exactly what I did, and what I hope you will do. I could turn an entire chapter from a review book, like First Aid, into digital flashcards in about 10 minutes.

By using digital information (e-books, PDF and PowerPoint files) and electronic flashcards I virtually eliminated all the time-consuming tasks of making flashcards (making, sorting, finding cards I needed, having the cards physically on hand when I had free time to study, etc....).

The results began to show. My total time spent on medical school related activities went from 12 hours a day to 2-3 hours a day, while my test scores and long-term retention of the valuable material shot up exponentially. Studying became more fun, and I actually looked forward to the daily "flashing" sessions.

The Flashcard Cookbook: How to Turn Information Into Perfect Electronic Flashcards

Rather than spend any more time talking about the theory of electronic flashcards, I'm going to jump right in and give you the step-by-step method to create your own perfect electronic flashcards. I have also created videos that show you EXACTLY what to do, so that you can follow along visually after you get the basic concepts. To access the videos, just join the free members-only online community for students who are reading this book at: www.facebook.com/studycoachmd.

Step 1: Prepare your Ingredients

Before getting started, you're going to need to collect the information you chose to study from in section II, and ideally, to find the electronic versions of this information. If you're using lecture notes, or slides from lecture, most of this can be found on your medical school student online portal in PDF and PowerPoint formats. If not, you'll need to find a way to scan the information quickly to make a digital copy.

If you're using textbooks, you usually have two options. If you already have the hard copy of the book, most medical textbooks have online companion sites (such as www.studentconsult.com for Goljan's pathology book). If you haven't already bought the book, it's best to buy an e-book copy, which is available on sites like Amazon's Kindle Store.

If neither of these options is available, search for your book on Google Scholar, or do a Google search for your book followed by the word "PDF" or "e-book" to see if there is a digital copy out there. I haven't yet come across a situation where I couldn't find the information I wanted to use digitally. Often, medical school libraries will also have electronic digital versions of many textbooks.

In the event you can't find a digital version of what you want to study, use a rapid double-sided scanner like the Fujitsu ScanSnap to create an electronic version.

Step 2: Choose a High Quality Flashcard Program

There are probably over 100 programs out there, and I've tried most of the most popular ones for Mac—

iFlash, Mental Case, Anki, iFlipr, Flashcard Exchange, etc.... After reading the medical student online forums and talking with other flashcard users, it seems that the general consensus for the Mac is iFlash. I haven't found a program with ALL these features yet for the PC, but from what I have seen, I think Anki appears to work best.

(If you find something better, please email me at dave@studycoachmd.com).

While the screencasts I use in the next section are based off the program iFlash, the principles behind each of these steps can be applied to any program that has similar features (listed below). I don't think the IDEAL program exists just yet, and I'm trying to make one myself now, but in the meantime, with a few tweaks of the settings, we can make these programs do exactly what we need them to do. When choosing a program, my recommendation is that it has these features:

1. Able to easily attach screenshot images: Usually, the programs that work have an "image" part of the front and back of a flashcard, and if you click on that area and "paste" your image, it should show up in that image portion.

2. You control the rate of repetition: Many programs such as Anki have a built in spaced repetition algorithm that chooses for you when you see and study certain cards. If you were a perfect student and used their formula religiously every day, this can work well. I like to have flexibility, and if I take a day off, I don't want an algorithm telling me what to do. So if possible, choose a program that lets you choose which cards you want to study and when you want to study them.

3. Learn how to take a screenshot and have it copied directly to the keyboard: While this is actually very easy and available on most computers, most people don't know how to do this. Usually your computer has a default command to take a screenshot and automatically "copy" it to your electronic clipboard. For the mac, this is Apple + Shift + Ctrl + 4. However, you can customize this keyboard command to make it more user-friendly. Check the website (www.facebook.com/studycoachmd) for a quick video tutorial of how to change your computers settings to make an easy screenshot. Note that the default file type of images in the mac is "png." This works well for most all programs, however if for some reason you want to change it to a jpg (such as for the Anki program), on a Mac, use Spotlight (the hourglass at the top right of the screen), and type in "Terminal" to find and then open the application called "Terminal." Once open, copy and paste this text without the parentheses (defaults write com.apple.screencapture type jpg) and hit enter. Then close Terminal, restart your computer, and voila!

Step 3: "Flash" your Material into Bite-Sized Chunks

As I mentioned earlier, most students use flash cards as a very small add-on to their normal study system of reading and taking notes. But, if it's such a powerful tool, why waste time reading and taking notes when we can turn everything we want to learn into flashcards? Reading alone is a mostly passive process, but when you combine reading using flashcards, you turn it into a very active learning process.

Unfortunately, this first step of turning your material, be it a book chapter or lecture notes, into flashcards is a mostly mindless process, but the good news is that it is extremely fast, and once you get going, you should be able to turn a hour-long lecture into cards in 2-3 minutes!

When you do this, remember you are not making flashcards of all your assigned readings; you are ONLY using the high yield information you identified in section II.

To get started, you're going to take screenshots of about a paragraph of text (or a fourth of a page) at a time, and paste that onto the back (or answer side) of your flashcard. This will take a little time to get used to at first, so be graceful with yourself while you get the hang of it. You may run into situations where a paragraph takes up 2/3 of the page. In this case, just choose a section of the paragraph to add to the flashcard, and overlap the next card with some of the text from the previous card (in the screencast video on the website (www.facebook.com/studycoachmd), I'll cover all these examples and special exceptions).

When you come across images with labels, the best thing to do is to include the whole image on the back of the flashcard, and do a separate screenshot on the front of the card, which includes the image and the lines, but cuts out as many of the labels as possible (again, I'll include examples of this in the screencast videos). If you come across a slide of a gross anatomy, gross pathology, histology, microbiology, etc.... image, then you'll nearly always want to paste this image onto the FRONT (or question side) of the flashcard. This is because, in most test situations, and real-life situations, you'll see the image in the question and have to answer a question related to it.

An important point to remember here is that YOU ARE NOT READING THE PARAGRAPHS when you do this.

You are simply and very QUICKLY capturing screenshots of the paragraphs and pasting them onto your cards. You will feel the temptation to make sure your cards are "right," by reading the paragraph, but remember that you really can't go wrong.

There are many ways to turn your material into perfect flashcards, so it's much better to get through the material fast.

When you're done, you should have converted your learning source, be it a book chapter, lecture notes, PowerPoint, etc. into a "deck" of flashcards with screenshots of information on the back, and nothing on the front (unless you have an unlabeled diagram or picture on the front as mentioned earlier). While you can make a whole weeks worth of cards in one sitting, I generally recommend just "flashing" one section at a time (i.e. one book chapter, one lecture, etc....).

Step 4: Write Personalized Questions

Now that your cards are filled with an "answer," it's time to write the questions, or the front of the cards. To get started, we'll work with small "stacks" of 5-8 flashcards at a time. When you open the first card, set up iFlash so that half of your screen is taken up with the image part of the card, and the other half with the text part. Again, watch the video if this seems confusing.

As you read the paragraph of text for the FIRST TIME, think about what questions you might ask yourself that would be answered by the information in the paragraph. Most often you'll have multiple questions on the front side of your card that are covered by the paragraph on the back. As you read the paragraph, type your questions onto the text part of the card on the left side of your screen, and when you are done, simply copy and paste your questions to the front side of the card.

Here are some tips to keep in mind as you write your questions:

Less is More

Just because the information is on the paragraph, doesn't mean you need to memorize it all. You have unique strengths and weaknesses, and you may already know much of the information on the card. If you already know the whole paragraph, just skip it entirely and delete it, if only one sentence is new to you, write a question just about that sentence. When in doubt, be a minimalist, you can always add more later.

Focus on Mechanisms

Whenever possible, it's best to focus your attention on mechanisms... This answers the "why" of the question not just the "what." You know you're focusing on the mechanism when you can not only explain the answer to the question, but also the STEPS involved in getting to that answer.

For example—one of the complications of diabetes is neuropathy, but why? The MECHANISM involves the enzyme Aldose Reductase which converts glucose to sorbitol, and sorbitol is an osmotically active solute drawing water into cell membranes. An excess of glucose in the blood causes an excess of sorbitol, which can lead to too much water inside cells and then rupture of cell membranes causing cell death. This type of osmotic damage to Schwann cells causes demyelination of peripheral nerves and results in a sensorimotor peripheral neuropathy.

Knowing this MECHANISM may seem much more complicated than just memorizing "diabetes causes peripheral neuropathy" but it has many benefits. First of all, by knowing the mechanism, you are making your learning network much more complex—connecting diabetes to biochemistry, to physiology, to anatomy. Furthermore, once you know this mechanism, you can connect the same pathophysiology to other complications of diabetes resulting from the same mechanism. For example, diabetic retinopathy is caused by excess sorbitol damaging pericytes in the retina and causing microaneruysms.

As you learn to master the mechanisms behind diseases, you'll find that you have to study less and less to know the same amount, because you'll be able to apply the mechanisms you have mastered to a variety of situations, even situations you've never seen before. USMLE test writers love to test your understanding of mechanisms.

When you learn mechanisms, you are connecting your material to such a broad and rich network, that you'll get exponentially better learning results than if you simply memorized a list of the "what" without knowing "why." Also, this is how test-makers formulate test questions, so if you focus your flashcards on this from the beginning, you'll have a huge head start.

The Right Breadth

As you do this, you want your questions to be general enough so as to not totally give away the answer, but also specific enough to guide your mind toward the answer. I have found that it's usually best to err on the side of being more specific.

Use Shorthand

These cards are for you, and you can save a lot of time by making up your own shorthand in your questions. For example, instead of definition, you might write "def" or instead of "Mechanism of Action" write "MOA."

Have Fun

Again—these questions and cards are for your eyes only, so try to add a few questions that make you laugh when you see them. Get creative. For example, when learning the reproductive system, I'd write questions like, "baby pees on his face, what does he have?" (epispadias). Or "why is it better to take pills through your vagina?" (b/c it bypasses first-pass metabolism).

After you finish writing your questions for the each card, check for immediate recall. It's important in this process that you PHYSICALLY WRITE the answer to the questions.

Have some scratch paper next to your computer when you study (I like the bright yellow legal paper), and after you make the questions for a card, look at those questions and see if you can write the answer on paper.

Physically writing is important for two reasons:

- It helps to enrich your memory network more deeply with yet another sense (physical touch)

- It helps you to make sure you actually know the answer. It's easy to look at your questions and convince yourself that you know the answer. When you actually write it on paper, you can see clearly whether you know it or not.

If you don't know the answer, simply look at the back of the card, read the answer, and then actually write the answer on your scratch paper. Then look at the front of the card again and continue this process until you can write the correct answers to the questions you made. As you write, use a lot of space and paper, and use shorthand... This is scratch paper and will be thrown away, so let yourself be fast and messy. I like to use a good ballpoint pen because the ink flows faster and makes it easier to write.

Repeat this process for your first set of 5-8 cards until you can immediately recall each of them. Then move on to the next 5-8 cards.

Step 5: Study the Mini-Deck

After finishing your first set of 5-8 complete cards with questions and answers, study them as a group, ideally in a random (or "shuffled") order. Again, write down the answers as you look at the questions, and continue repeating the cards for as long as it takes until you can recall them all.

By now, you've seen and ACTIVLEY recalled the information on each card several times, and the material is well on its way to being permanently engraved in your long-term memory.

Step 6: Finish the Deck and Do a Comprehensive Review

Repeat steps 4 and 5, in small groups of cards (5-8 at a time), until you're done with the entire deck you created (most decks are 30-60 cards depending on how big a chapter you're doing).

After finishing the deck, grab a cup of coffee, or take a quick stretch break, because you're going to review the whole deck now. Set your flashcard program on shuffle, and this time you're going to shuffle the entire deck, studying ALL the cards in a random order.

If you can write the answer to a card on the first time, check it off as "known," and continue to the next card. For all the cards that you didn't get on the first time, "flag" them for later review (see screencast video for how to flag).

You will now move these "flagged" cards to a separate deck; I call mine "Keepers." But you could call yours "high yield" or whatever. The point is that this new deck represents a customized chunk of high yield information that is specific for your own learning needs. When it comes time to prepare for a test, instead of giving an equal amount of your time to all the study material as most students do before tests (even studying things they already know), you will be able to focus ONLY on what is uniquely high yield for you, simultaneously saving your hours of review, and increasing your mastery of the subject.

By now, through this focused active learning process, you have practically memorized whatever information you just studied. You have formed a rock solid memory network that you'll continue to refine and strengthen each time you quiz yourself.

Chapter 13: Understanding Why This Works

Returning to the beginning of this section, our goal was to find a learning system that worked with the brain in mind—a system that teaches you in the same way that your brain likes to learn.

Complex and Multi-Sensory From the Beginning

Electronic flashcards let you easily study both text and diagrams and pictures, which are processed in different areas of your brain. You can incorporate audio into the cards as well if you want (you can download MP3 heart sounds here: http://www.med.umich.edu/lrc/psb/heartsounds/index.htm). Also, when you physically write the answers on paper, you are linking the material to your physical touch, and your muscle memory. All of these senses are using different parts of your brain so you are effectively creating a neural network across the whole brain.

Connected to Pre-Existing Networks From the Beginning

This system is like the equivalent of designing your own curriculum.
You've not only chosen what unique sources you're going to study, but you choose what parts of those sources you'll focus on.

Furthermore, within each card, YOU choose the relevant parts and create your own individualized questions. This way, whatever you study is immediately linked to your pre-existing memory networks, and focused on your own unique learning needs---yielding exponentially greater learning results.

Finally, as you study, the system lets you to personalize the bite-sized chunks of information within your card deck, focusing the most attention on the information you know least, while less attention on that which you know best. You don't waste any time reviewing things you already know.

Novelty

Remember the importance of seeing material in a new way to keep your learning mechanisms intact? In this study method, each time you shuffle your cards, you are seeing the material in a different order, which forces you to be in the moment and think on your foot. These are the same skills you'll need to take timed exams and to be a great doctor.

Based on Spaced-Repetition

Flashcards are DESIGNED on the principle of spaced repetition, the proven mechanism for encoding long-term memory in the brain. You see the material first when you make the flashcards and write your custom questions, then again when you study them for the first time, then again in a different order when you review your entire deck, and then again as you flag the ones you know least and repeat them in your "high yield" deck! By the time you're done, you've seen and ACTIVELY RECALLED the same bits of information at least four times.

Active Learning

Unlike passively listening to a lecture, reading notes, or reading a book, this system is similar to a test in that it forces you to participate in the learning process by ACTIVELY RECALLING the information on each card. Each time you actively recall the answer to your questions, you turbo-charge your memory network. If reading notes to learn information is like 2 horsepower scooter engine, active recall and writing down your answers are like a jet propulsion engine.

Formatted Like a Test

It just makes sense to learn the material in a similar way to how you will be tested on it. If tests are in question-answer format, why not study that way? If tests have histology or pathology pictures and then ask you questions about that, why not study that way, incorporating those pictures directly into your cards? This is why students consistently say that their highest yield learning resources for Step 1 are question banks—simulated test questions like USMLE World or Kaplan QBank.

Fast

As you master copying and pasting, and screenshots, you'll be able to make flash cards FAR faster than you could make notes.

Searchable

Digital information is searchable... Let's say you realized you're a bit weak in the topic of "osteomyelitis", just search it using spotlight (mac), or Google desktop (pc), and your flashcard files containing that term will show up for you in seconds, ready for you to review!

Portable

Just like the first iPod's advertisement was "one thousand songs in your pocket," think of flashcards as "one thousand flashcards in your backpack." This means that you can study nearly anywhere without the hassle of carrying around heavy books or gathering up your notes. Many of the flashcard programs also have companion mobile apps for the iPhone, iPad, Android, etc.... I haven't found that these work great yet with cards with images (aka screenshots) attached, however I imagine this will be worked out in the near future.

Sharable

If you want to work with friends, it is very easy to work together to make high quality cards and share them. Be careful when you do this, because you usually lose the "personalized" factor when you share them. But this can be especially helpful when using cards for review before a test, because the novelty of other people's cards will help you to think of the material in a different way, which may be the way it is on the test!

Definite Endpoint

Another thing I love about flashcards is that there is no ambiguity of whether you're done or not. With reviewing notes or re-reading book chapters, you can read them over an infinite amount of times and never have a clear sense of when you're done. With flashcards, using active recall, you either know the information on your cards or you don't. You're done once you know your cards. It's that simple.

Comprehensive

This system allows for nearly all your sources of information to be processed in one place. You can add information from books, lectures, the internet, labs, review sessions, practice tests, and capture it all for review using the same system.

Congratulations!!!

At this point of the book, you are nearly done. You've zoomed out and looked at the medical school experience, how it's designed, and how it intersects with your own goals and vision for your life. You then filtered down the huge amount of potential learning sources into only the highest quality small amount of information that you decided to start learning. And now in this chapter, you learned the some practical information about how the brain learns best as well as the nitty gritty details about a study process that works in line with the brain to give you maximal efficiency and maximal productivity.

After putting this study system into practice, you should begin to feel the exhilaration of learning so much in such a short time, and should be starting to enjoy your ever-increasing amount of free time! Take some time (a week or 2) to put this study system into practice before moving on. The rest of the book will focus on fine-tuning this system as well as some additional tips for test prep. See you then!

Section IV: Fine Tuning Your Learning System

I like to think of learning something new as building a skyscraper in your mind. You start by working with an architect to design your building. This is what we did in section I where you got clear about your goals and chose high quality building materials.

Next, you build the steel frame of a building, the basic structure that supports your edifice of knowledge. You did this by selecting customized learning sources, priming yourself, connecting the dots, and writing customized questions on your flashcards.

Next, construction workers will pour concrete around those steel beams, shaping them into a strong foundation that can even withstand an earthquake. You did this, the bulk of your learning, with your first rounds of studying your electronic flashcards, thus engraining their information in your short and intermediate term memory.

By now, the bulk of your metaphorical memory skyscraper is complete.
All that's left to do are the finishing touches, sealing the cracks, painting the walls, putting in the lights, the tile, the windows, decorating the rooms, etc.... This is what we're going to focus on in this section.

I'll talk about how to seal the cracks in your knowledge, and then we'll go into how to design an optimal study environment as well as how long to study and how to schedule your study periods. Of course, you don't need to follow all of this advice, but these are all small practicalities that many students have found very useful.

By practicing what you learn in this section in addition to what you've already learned up to this point, your skyscraper of knowledge will be complete down to the minutest detail. And as you get an even deeper understanding of this study system and will begin to perfect it and further customize it for your own learning style and learning needs.

Chapter 14: Finding the Cracks

Before moving on to the interior decorating of your memory skyscraper, I want to make sure that there aren't any cracks in the foundation. As you learn, you'll want to make sure you are aware of any gaps in your knowledge so that you can then seal them promptly and effectively. Have you ever had a tiny crack in your car's windshield? What happened to it over time? How about a small tear in your jeans? What happened to that if you didn't fix it? The same thing happens with gaps in your knowledge. If you let these gaps persist, they will grow and grow, and when test-time comes around, you'll likely miss several questions you could have easily gotten had you addressed your knowledge gaps earlier. Instead, I'll teach you a way to easily find these cracks and seal them in an efficient and productive way.

As you go through the first rounds of studying your flashcards, I want you to pay specific attention to the mechanisms (the "why" question), and notice when things don't make sense, or when some part of the information is missing. In our previous example about diabetes, we learned the mechanism of how hyperglycemia can cause neuropathy and retinopathy. However, as you study, you'll also learn that uncontrolled diabetes also causes nephropathy, or kidney damage. When you ask yourself "why" you'll learn that this occurs by a completely different mechanism. Instead of osmotic damage from excess sorbitol, hyperglycemia damages the kidneys through non-enzymatic glycosylation of basement membrane proteins. This causes structural damage to the glomerulus, causing it to leak protein.

At first, finding these missing pieces in your knowledge might seem like it is inefficient, but as you practice this, you'll be amazed at how an initial investment of time and energy pays off in the long run, and you'll be able to learn and understand things much faster. Again, with the above example, now that you know about the process of non-enzymatic glycosylation, you can understand conceptually what Hemoglobin A1C is, and why this lab can give you information about glucose levels for 120 days.

The goal at first is just to IDENTIFY your questions or learning gaps, and RECORD them somewhere that works for you. It's actually inefficient and distracting to continually stop studying to look up the answers to your questions one at a time. Instead, I suggest keeping your questions in a list on paper, a word document, Evernote, or in an iPhone "note" file, whatever works best for you. Later, we'll go over what to do with those questions.

For example, I use the program Evernote to track these questions. I just have a note in my shortcuts called "Study Questions" and if I'm at my computer I just write bullet points of my questions as I go through a study session. If I'm listening to a lecture or review tape when I'm out running or in the car (and obviously don't have pen/paper/computer), I'll just use the "voice memo" function on the Evernote app on my iPhone to add a voice note to the "Study Questions" to make sure I record my question. Some people who are less "techy" prefer to record these learning gaps in a small notebook. Regardless of what you use, it's important to have a system that works for you and your style.

Process: Finding the Cracks

Perhaps just reflecting on this right now, you already have a list of questions identifying your learning gaps. If so, make sure you have them all together on an easy-to-access list. If not, during your next study session or review session, get as curious as you can about what you're learning and make sure you can answer "why?" to most of the flashcard questions you come across. If there are concepts you're missing, take note of them on your list.

Before moving onto the next section, make sure you have a list of at least 5 questions identifying "cracks" in your knowledge skyscraper.

Chapter 15: Sealing the Cracks

After you've started to notice the cracks in your memory skyscraper, it's time to fill them in with concrete. The previous step showed you how to identify gaps in your knowledge. These next few points should give you some ideas on how to get your questions answered as efficiently as possible. Here are some ideas:

Ask the Professor

This is probably the best way to seal the cracks, as you'll get the best answers and it's the most efficient. Since I didn't learn well from live lecture (and so rarely went to class), I would just email my professors a list of questions whenever I had a few. Make sure they go to the right person though—i.e. don't email the question about antibiotics to your anatomy teacher. If you do go to class, ask your professor during or after class.

Both of these methods not only help you seal your information cracks, but also help you develop a personal relationship with your professor, which is not only beneficial for your future career but also helps make the school experience more fun.

Some medical schools have much more interactive classes designed for Q&A sessions like this, which would be a perfect place to bring your list of learning gaps.

Ask a Smart Friend

Another option is to save up these questions for a study group with smart friends. Simply by discussing them in a group, you'll not only answer your questions, but you'll most likely discover other tid-bits of information to seal other cracks you didn't even know existed. Also you friends will probably be happy because you will be providing material for starting your study groups.

Look it Up

You should be able to get nearly all your questions answered well and fast using the above two strategies, but if for some reason those don't work, you can always resort to the time-tested strategy of looking it up. Wikipedia will be there for you 24/7, and often helps with low-yield questions you are just curious about but don't want to bother your teachers or friends about.

You might find, as I did, that as you become more aware of mechanisms, and get into the habit of asking "why," you'll start to get more curious about things in general. For example, one day I started to wonder why it was that so many American's are obese. That led me down the road of learning about neuropeptides, high fructose corn syrup, the mechanism of addictions, the Kaiser ACE study, and US agricultural policies from started after World War II.

These sorts of random facts may seem irrelevant, but remember from the last section about the brain--the more you can connect the material to your life, your previous memory networks, your emotions, and your innate curiosity, the stronger the new learning networks will be!

Process: Sealing the Cracks

Ok, now take your list of questions from step 1, and using the bullet points above as a guide, choose where you want to get your questions answered, and ask away.

Once you get the answers to your gaps, DON'T STOP THERE! Take these answers and make quick flash cards about them.

You could make a deck called "gaps," or "questions" or "cracks" or whatever you want. Add your questions and answers to your deck of cards and study them just like you would with your core material. As you get used to this system, you'll soon realize that these cards are very high yield, and you'll want to combine them in your final "keeper" or "flagged" deck to review again before the test.

With the cracks sealed, you're ready to start painting, putting in the windows and tile, and furnishing your memory skyscraper. In our learning metaphor, this means taking a look at where and when to study.

Chapter 16: Setting Up Your Macro Environment

I love going to the library to see how many people are passed out on top of their textbooks and notes. It seems that people feel as if they're on task when they're in the library, like they're putting in their time, and whether they study well there or not, they at least feel productive and can tell their friends—"I spent 6 hours in the library today." I remember one day before finals in college (before I knew about or practiced any of these techniques), some friends and I spent the entire night in the library (yeah, I was that cool). We literally snuck in pillows and blankets, camped up in a room on the 13th floor, and "studied" all day and night. It was a great memory and we had a lot of fun, but it goes without saying that we didn't study very well there.

Most students choose to study in the library by default, without necessarily trying out different environments. How do you feel when you think about going to the library? What images come up in your mind? If you're like most people, this isn't a place you're particularly excited about going. It's not necessarily an exciting experience, and more than likely it seems like drudgery, or an obligation to go there.

I'm not saying to write-off the library entirely. It can be very convenient if you happen to be on campus, need free Wi-Fi, want to be around friends and colleagues, or if you truly are the type of person who needs absolute quiet to study. But before you put yourself in this box, let me talk about some of the benefits of doing just the opposite—studying in a loud environment.

Why to Study in a Loud Place

Most people think they need to be in a totally quiet environment to study, but rarely is this the case. More often than not, these people would actually study better and have more fun in different environments, but they just haven't given it an honest try. The cultural norm for studying is a quiet place like the library, and most people get used to this. But, just because you've always studied like this, doesn't mean it's the best way for you. It may be, but it may not be. Here are two reasons to try studying in a louder place.

The first is that it has a beneficial side effect of developing your attention and ability to focus. If you become good at re-directing your focus to what you are studying even while there are conversations and noises going on around you, you set yourself free. You will eventually be able to study anywhere (i e. airports, on buses, on planes, coffee shops, etc....), turning otherwise wasted time into productive learning time.

Furthermore, when you take tests in the future, and the person next to you has a sniffling nose and the guy behind you keeps tapping his foot on the ground, you won't be distracted by it and can easily continue to focus on the exam without this bothering you. You'll find that studying in loud environments is actually easier using the study system outlined in this book because it demands nearly 100% of your focus. It's easy to get distracted when you're passively reading a book or reading over notes, but when you are forcing yourself to write down answers to questions in front of you, it's much harder to multi-task.

The second reason to try this out is that, in general, louder places are simply more FUN. I personally love studying in coffee shops because they are lively and usually full of interesting people doing interesting things (for example, in LA, it seems like everyone's working on reading or writing screenplays). They usually have lots of light, artwork on the walls, smells of fresh coffee and pastries; free Wi-Fi, and good music!

Other places to consider are studying outside or studying at a friend's house. This is different than a group study session. By this I mean you are each studying on your own but happen to be next to each other. A group study session has different purposes, which are usually better during the review phase, but studying alongside your buddies can make the process more fun and you can always hang out and chat on your study breaks.

If you try this out, you'll likely find that you can rapidly teach yourself to focus in a noisy environment and you'll start to see the benefits of this skill as early as your next test. But even if you never get used to the noise, the main thing to take away from this section is to choose study environments that are fun to YOU, and that you'll look forward to going to.

Why to Study in a Different Place

Try to remember one of your first trips to a new place; such as the first time you visited your college. Can you picture it in your mind--the way the streets looked, the smells, the strange language that people may have been speaking, the temperature, the color of the flowers on the sides of the street, the taste of the new foods? Your mind is probably wandering through all sorts of wonderful memories by now. Now, try to remember the first Tuesday of last month (assuming you were at home).

Even though you can remember your trips to new places in exquisite detail, it's likely you can't remember much if anything from that random Tuesday a few weeks ago! This is because our brains are designed to be adaptive. We are on high alert when we're outside of our comfort zone, in a new environment. Our brains become alive and activated. However, even after a few times at a "new" place, we can become accustomed to the surroundings. This natural habit of the mind can be helpful at times because it allows us to feel safe and at home in places we already know about, but it also can blunt our sensory awareness and brain power when we want to be learning.

By studying in NEW environments, we can harness this power of the mind to heighten awareness and give an easy sensory boost to whatever memory network we are trying to build. The best way to understand this is through experience, so give it a try!

Process: Making it Fun and New

Now it's time to give these strategies a try!

Get on Yelp (www.yelp.com) and search for "study spots" near your current location. Use the "filters" feature to add "Free Wi-Fi" and/or whatever else you want to your search. Look at the places with the best reviews and check them out. Think about combining a study session or 2 with something else in that area that would be fun for you (i.e. surfing, rock climbing, a hike, movie, whatever!).

If you absolutely must have a library, try a different place. Again, get on Yelp (www.yelp.com) and search for libraries near your current location. A lot of times, going to a public library can be quite and still much more fun than your school's library.

As you go to these places, sit in different seats, study with someone you don't usually study with. Keep changing your routine. Remember the key is to DO SOMETHING DIFFERENT!

When you're studying using Audio—you have total freedom of location. Like I mentioned in the last section, you can easily study in the car, while running, at the gym, or while cooking or cleaning. I even listened to Goljan while snowboarding in

Utah, hiking volcanoes in Nicaragua, or while on a 12 hour hike in Southern Chile!

At least 2 times this week, commit to spending at least 1.5 – 2 hours studying in NEW places and new places within those places. Remember, the goal is to get into the habit of keeping your study environments NEW and FUN (and don't be afraid if the places are noisy!) The opportunities are boundless.

120

Chapter 17: Setting Up Your Microenvironment

We already talked about how most students "pay attention" in class. If you haven't noticed this already, for your next class, sit in the very back row and take a look around. How many laptops are open to ESPN, GChat, Facebook, etc.? How many students are having their own conversations on the side? At my school, I'd say 75% were doing this, and 25% (at the most) were actually paying full attention to the lecture and their notes.

Now, watch these same students study outside of class. I have many friends that "study" while watching their favorite TV show or take unscheduled breaks every 10 minutes to talk on the phone. The typical student at my school would simultaneously "study," check email, download new songs, be in several internet conversations and text conversations, and be in the middle of at least 3 different games of "Words with Friends" on their iPhones.

While I appreciate the quest to do many things at once, unfortunately our brains just don't work well with this set-up. We end up thinking we're "studying" but in reality we are putting in a lot of hours and not getting a lot done. The brain is physically not capable of focusing on more than one completely different information network at once.

What's really going on in your skull is that when you study, your dorsolateral prefrontal cortex (DLPFC) is filled with whatever you're studying. Then when your phone beeps with a new message and you check it, your brain literally DROPS all that info (before it goes to your hippocampus to be coded into your long-term memory) and your brain spends a lot of energy to load your text message into your DLPFC. Then this happens again when you focus on your TV show, or your Words with Friends Game, or whatever! Each of these mental switches takes time and energy to stop and then re-start, creating a very inefficient system.

In fact, studies show that when you are interrupted in a task, it not only takes 50% longer to get something done, but there are also 50% more errors on what you're doing! If this happens while you're studying, you might do 50% worse than you want to on your exam. But if this happens later while you're practicing medicine, someone could die. When you start your clinical years, you'll notice that most nurses have the medication cabinet (the PIXIS station) in a separate quiet room where they can focus on their patient's medications without being interrupted. This system was put into place after a review committee noticed the amount of errors that happened when people would interrupt nurses while they worked.

Whereas a new LOCATION is actually beneficial to your learning (because it doesn't require your direct attention, but instead activates your peripheral attention and level of awareness), having multiple things in your microenvironment that demand your DIRECT attention will make your learning very inefficient.

Have you ever had moments in the past when you were studying or working so intensely that time seemed to stop, and the next thing you know 1 or 2 hours had passed? When you focus on a single thing (in this case studying), your brain starts to build up inertia, like a snowball rolling down a hill and picking up speed. The longer you focus, the easier it is to focus, and this process continues until you hit a natural break point.

Psychologist Mihaly Csikszentmihalyi, one of the world's top researchers in creativity and happiness, called this state "Flow" and found that when employees are in this state, they experience their greatest life satisfaction. This is one of the reasons why when you learn to study the way I'm teaching you, you'll find it will actually be fun and fulfilling! And you'll actually have time to hang out with your friends rather than just texting them!

To help yourself create this state of "flow," you need to start by controlling your microenvironment—all of the things in your line of sight that might take away your attention.

Remove YOUR Distractions

Not everyone has the same distractions, and only you know what yours are. For example, I've trained myself to be able to study very well in coffee shops, and although I occasionally do some people watching, I'm able to do so without really losing focus on what I'm studying. On the other hand, I know that if my phone rings, or if my e-mail program bounces up and down letting me know I have a new message, that's much harder to ignore, and I'll usually stop whatever I was studying to check the message.

So, be aware of what your distractions are, and for the time period you set to study (more about this later), turn off the phone, turn off the email program, close the web-browser, do whatever it takes to eliminate your most potent distractions. Also, most flashcard programs (including iFlash) have the ability to go into full screen mode, so all you can see on your screen is the program. This makes it easy to remove distractions from your computer. (Note, to do this in iFlash, just push the letter "H" while you're in study mode).

Process: Setting Up the Microenvironment

After reading the section above, get out a piece of paper (or open up a Word doc) and take 5-10 minutes to reflect on what YOUR main distractions are while you study. Be honest with yourself! If you're having a hard time, just think about the past few study sessions you had and think about what was most distracting. Here are some common distractions:

- Noises or Vibrations from your Phone
- New E-Mails
- Messages like texts, G-Chat, iMessage, etc....
- Social Media: Facebook, Instagram, etc....
- Conversations from people sitting near you
- Papers on your desk representing things you have to do (i.e. mail or bills)
- Applications on your computer trying to tell you something.

Whatever comes up for you, think about how you can minimize these when you study. Again, this will take some experimenting to see what works best for you. So try a few strategies out and see what sticks. Try turning off your phone, shutting down your email program, and closing chat programs just while you're in a study session. Maybe close down any apps you aren't using and hide your application doc. Maybe study in full screen mode, so all you can see is what you're studying. If you're at home, study at a clean desk; if you're at a coffee shop, and people's conversations bug you, try music. More on that later...

Chapter 18: How to Study

Rock On

Listening to music while studying not only helps make your learning experience more complex and multi-sensory, but it also happens to facilitate the type of learning you do in medical school. Wait—didn't I JUST say not to distract yourself? Yes, but in this case, the music is not something you're focusing directly on, but will be happening in the background while your attention stays focused on what you're studying.

Music is one of those things, like studying outside of the library, that most students don't believe that they can do while studying. Again, the truth is that most students just haven't tried it long enough to really know if it helps or not. Remember those studies your parents told you about how learning music helps us to learn math and science? They weren't kidding. For some reason, the logical left-brain systems that we use to learn science, or medicine, work even better when we simultaneously listen to music.

If this is new to you, start by listening to music without lyrics. My personal favorite is to listen to techno or house music on Pandora, because the fast pace energies me while I study. I also like some of the study playlists on Spotify. Again, try it for a few study sessions a week for about a month, and then re-evaluate. Eventually, you'll likely find that you can listen to anything and still focus on what you're studying. In fact you'll likely focus even better!

If you listen to music, you also help to tune out distracting conversations happening around you (which can sometimes be distracting if you study in coffee shops). You can also use it as a time to check out new artists you've wanted to hear!

So, for at least 2 study sessions this week, try studying with music. If this is new to you, start with music without lyrics at a low volume. If you've done that but have never tried music with lyrics, try that. Remember to keep your primary focus on the flashcards and what you're studying and just let the music play in the background.

Groups—When to and When Not to Study Alone

If you made it to medical school, you probably don't have very fond memories of group projects from high school or college, because it was likely you doing all the work. However, in med school you're surrounded by an incredibly intelligent crowd of people, and studying in groups, when used right, can be of enormous benefit.

In general, it's best to avoid groups when you're building the frame of your learning network, because that's when you're doing the heavy duty learning of getting the concepts down. Because people learn so differently, and because you'll each have a different amount of base knowledge, your conversations in a group during this phase of learning won't be very helpful. I learned this right away during my first gross anatomy labs. We tried to study as a group, but we were all seeing the material for the first time... "I THINK the lungs end at the 6th rib, but I'm not sure," "Really? I thought they ended at the 8th?" We ended up just guessing at things during our dissection. The, one person would usually stumble through the dissection guide and read the right answer if they could find it. This type of group studying was somewhat fun because we were in a group but wasn't helpful at all. In fact, it was actually harmful because when guess about information like that, we run the risk of inadvertently memorizing incorrect information. If you're not sure if you have accurate study material, you're better off NOT hearing/discussing/thinking about this information at all!

Instead, the time to use group studying is during the REVIEW phase of your learning, NOT when you're building your initial learning framework. After you think you know the information inside and out, organize a group with your smartest friends and have everyone show up to the group with specific questions targeting each of your learning gaps (that you identified earlier in this section). Now, when you meet in a group and talk about specific questions, you will all be highly informed and can explain concepts to each other in a NEW way, thus strengthening and solidifying your learning network while you fill in the gaps. Also, trying to teach and explain what you think you know to your friends, you'll be able to see clearly how well you really know the material, and you may find further learning gaps that need to review more (which you'll add to your learning gap list of course!)

My gross anatomy group eventually figured this out and decided to review the dissection study guide IN DETAIL the day before the dissection. Because attendance at this lab was mandatory, we decided to maximize the time we spent there since we had to be there anyway. So we would each master the material the night before, pretending that the dissection lab was the final test. Then, during the lab the following day, we connected our book knowledge of the anatomy, physiology, and pathology that we studied before to the visual, tactile, multi-sensory experience of the dissection itself to boost and strengthen our learning networks. While we did the dissection, we would teach each other, reviewing what we had studied, and covering any learning gaps we had. This process was SO productive and efficient, that after we started doing this, we would usually only review 1-3 hours before the final exam, and all of us got test scores in the high 90's! Try this out with your own gross anatomy group!

Before moving on, I want to take a moment to re-visit the distinction between studying in the same LOCATION as your friends from an actual GROUP STUDY session. The former is great to do even at the initial stages of building your learning network because it can make your study sessions more fun. In this scenario, you are each studying your OWN material at your OWN pace during your study sessions. For example, you might both be at a table at a coffee shop together, but you're each engaged in your own work and not talking to each other. Then, when it is time for a break, your friends are right there to chat with or have lunch with. In contrast the GROUP STUDY session is something I recommend you do during the final review sessions before a test, or during mandatory labs (such as the gross anatomy example above) in order to maximize the time you have to spend there anyway.

Chapter 19: How Long to Study

In real estate, the motto is "location, location, location." In the realm of learning, it's "timing, timing, timing!" Most medical students end up studying too long. Have you ever noticed that after a certain period of studying, you start to get diminishing returns, you are more distractible, and you might even get in a bad mood and have to completely stop for several hours before even thinking about studying again?

This is no coincidence. Studies and experience show that you can only really keep your attention on something for a limited period of time—usually between 50 minutes to a couple hours. Of course you can force yourself to keep going, but usually that will have devastating consequences and you'll get burnt out on studying for the day.

For me, I know am able to study well for about 90 minutes to 2 hours. Sometimes I can keep going for 3 hours, but then usually I'll hit a wall and burn out, get in a bad mood, and have to stop for the day or take a LONG break before I can study again. On the other hand, if I stop myself at 2 hours maximum (even if I'm still feeling good) and then take a 30-minute break, I can keep this cycle up all day if I need to.

The goal is to study in short but highly focused bursts of energy. This will not only help you maximize the learning output of your time, creating more free time, but it will also help your study experience be more enjoyable and invigorating by creating a "flow" experience. The study method of this book, using active learning of electronic flashcards, lends itself naturally to this intense level of focus, so you should have no problem putting this principle to practice.

Have a Time Goal vs. a Subject Goal

Have you ever sat down to study and said to yourself—"I'm going to stay here until I finish chapter X," or "I'm going to do 200 practice questions a day." Did you notice yourself being inpatient, always in the back of your mind thinking—"as soon as I finish this chapter I can get out of here." When you have a goal to do a chunk of work, whether it's reviewing a chapter, or a day's worth of notes, your mind can easily confuse the goal of getting through the session with the goal of actually LEARNING that material. Our brains have built in reward circuitry, and your brain can't help but to rush you through your defined task in order to get your reward whether that's break time, or giving yourself a good feeling because you've done a "day's work."

Instead, you can use that same reward circuitry to benefit your learning by setting a TIME Goal rather than a SUBJECT goal for each study session. The goal is to study and learn for a set amount of TIME, regardless of how much of the chapter you finish. When you do this, you'll notice your unconscious mind won't try to rush you through the material, and instead, you can really let yourself dive into the material and get curious for a predetermined amount of time. As I mentioned in the previous section, the exact amount of time may differ for each person, but a good starting point is between 1.5 to 2 hours per study session.

The other benefit of having a time goal is you create a positive emotional feedback loop. As long as you put in the time you told yourself you'd do, you "succeeded" in your goals for that day and your mind will reward you with positive feelings and improved self-esteem. You'll feel good about yourself and inspired to continue to grow in your learning. Over time, this creates a positive emotional feedback loop in relation to studying which will help to motivate you to study in the future.

On the other hand, if you use the old system of creating goals based on subjects, not only will you feel rushed and hurried to get your chapter or question-set done, but if you don't happen to get through it for whatever reason, you'll likely beat yourself up, feel stressed, and overwhelmed, creating a downward emotional feedback loop.

So why not choose the positive emotions? As you get in the habit of doing this, you'll likely notice that it becomes easier and easier to enter into that timeless "flow" state. I often have to set a little timer on my phone or computer to buzz after 90 minutes to remind me to stop.

Why Stop? The Importance of Scheduling Breaks

Now, you might think it makes sense that if you're feeling really good studying, to just keep going and going, right?

Wrong. This type of studying is the mental equivalent of a sprint, using 100% focus and energy for short bursts of time. If a runner tries to sprint a marathon, she'll burn out very quickly; if you run a car at full throttle for a road-trip, the engine will die; and if you try to study at full blast forever, your study session will come to an abrupt halt with you feeling so drained and burnt out that you'll have to take a very long break or stop studying altogether for that day in order to reset your system.

This brings us to the importance of taking scheduled breaks at set intervals in order to keep your mental engine well-oiled and able to work for you for as many study bursts as you want it to. As I mentioned above, you may actually not WANT to stop studying when break time comes up, but it's important to STOP ANYWAY, before your engine runs out and it's too late. Like I did, you may want to set a timer when you sit down to study to remind you that it's break-time.
In general, if a study session is usually between 60-120 minutes, I recommend a 20-30 minute break between study sessions and a larger break after doing 2-3 sessions. In your break, it's INTEGRAL to totally switch mental gears and do something different. This is not the time to look up answers to questions you had while studying or to email professors with school related things.

This is the time to completely switch gears. Open up your email, turn on your phone, open Facebook and GChat, read the news, look at that funny video on YouTube that your friend sent you. Or go for a walk, grab a bite to eat, go shopping at a store nearby, whatever. The point is that the break-time is spent with something different from studying, and that YOU experience it as fun and energizing. After 30 minutes, you should feel rejuvenated and ready, if not looking forward to, another study session.

After completing a few study sessions (usually 2-3) with breaks in between, your brain will usually need a longer break to recharge. This is an ideal time to do some exercise, as it will not only help to rejuvenate and reenergize you, but will also help you seal in the memory networks you just worked on and prime your brain with BDNF and Nitric Oxide for your next study session.

Process: Creating Your Perfect Study Session

Now it's time to put these principles into practice to set up the ideal study session for YOU.

Step 1: Find Your Mental Sprint Time

The first step is to find the right amount of time for your study sessions. Sprinters typically will choose the distance that they do best, and train for this type of competition whether it's the 100m, 200m, or 400m race. Similarly, your mind will naturally have a baseline mental sprinting capacity it does best.

To find this, start by trying to be aware of your level of mental engagement during the next few times you sit down to study. Notice your build-up of mental energy as you get into your material, and then notice when you start to think about other things and get distracted. Consider starting a timer when you start studying, and periodically glace down at it when you notice your mental energy starting to diminish. You'll likely find that this time period will be between 60min – 120min. If in doubt, start with 90 minutes and you can adjust accordingly later for what works best for you.

Step 2: Find Your Burnout Time

Hopefully you only need to experiment once or twice to discover your general mental burnout time. The purpose of this is to give you a mental concept of your maximum time. This information is helpful to know because there will be some times you may want to extend your study session a little longer than your usual time. If you know your burnout time, then you'll be aware of just how long you could extend your study session in special circumstances before you hit this point of no return.

To do this, choose a day when it would be ok if you didn't study at all. Set a timer when you sit down to study, and after getting into the "flow" zone of your study session, just let yourself keep on going and going until you burn out. Signs that you've hit this state are mental and physical exhaustion, feeling irritable or angry, and feeling like you have to get out of the study environment. Once you've hit it, take a look at your timer and keep a mental note of your personal burnout time.

Step 3: Learn What Rejuvenates You During Breaks

Take some time to experiment with what break time activities give you the most fun and rejuvenation. Again, apply Pareto's principle here. Which 20% of activities give you 80% of positive feelings and mental rejuvenation? If you don't know off the top of your head, experiment with different things. Maybe it's connection with other people (calling a friend, texting, email, Facebook, online chat programs). Maybe it's watching an episode of your favorite TV show. Maybe it's reading a novel. Maybe it's playing music. Maybe it's meditating! You may even want to create a fun "get to do" list. This would be either a physical or digital list of some fun and/or mindless things you'd like to do. If there are times during your day when you come across something you'd like to check out, add it to this list, so that you have a bunch of ideas waiting for you when break time comes around.

Step 4: Putting it All Together

Now it's time to start to put it all together. Choose a day you have unscheduled, and then choose a fun and new location to study. After getting set up, get your timer out and study at 100% focus for your pre-determined amount of time, meeting your "time goal."

When your timer goes off, STOP (even if you want to keep going), and set your timer for 20-30min for your break time and get busy doing all of the fun things that rejuvenate you.

When the timer goes off again, shut down the distractions (phone, email, Facebook, etc....) and get started on your next study session for your pre-determined amount of time.

When your timer goes off again, you can either choose to leave to a new location and take a bigger break, or if you're feeling great, try to do another schedule break and a final study session.

For most people, the limit at each location is between 2-4 study sessions. However, remember, that by the time you put all these principles from this book into practice, you'll likely only need to do 1-2 study sessions each day to master the material.

Chapter 20: Schedule Your Days and Weeks With Parkinson's Law

Cyril Northcote Parkinson, born in the early 20th century, was a British naval historian most famous for his hysterical book, Parkinson's Law[6], which details many of his observations of government bureaucracies*. His concluding thesis was the "law" that "work expands to fill the time available for it's completion."

This is similar to the scientific principle that a gas will expand to fill whatever size container you put it in. Parkinson noticed that if people were given a relatively simple job but a long time to complete it, they would turn it into a difficult job and end up using all of the time they were given to complete the job.

Think about yourself in college. Have you ever had a long-term project such a senior thesis? Did the workload of that assignment expand to fill the amount of time you had for it?

Parkinson's law can also be seen if you have a lot of free time. Think about a time in the summer when you only had a couple of errands to run. Likely those errands seemed like huge insurmountable tasks that might even take a whole day to complete. Just like a gas expands to fill whatever size box you put it in, a task will expand to fill any chunk of time you give it.

This is incredibly important to grasp for this study system, because even if you have only the highest quality information and learn to study very efficiently--if you are WILLING to give your whole day to studying, it will still fill your whole day.

On the other hand, if you do the opposite and only allow yourself a small amount of time to get a task done, the task will seem much easier to complete. You will minimize any

---

[6] Parkinson, C. (1957). Parkinson's law, and other studies in administration. Boston: Houghton Mifflin.

unnecessary complexity and your brain will focus much more efficiently on getting the most important things done, after all there isn't much time for anything else!

Everyone knows the truism that if you really want a task to be completed, assign it to the busiest person you know. This is because that person is only willing or able to give a small amount of time to that task, and consequently the workload of the task decreases significantly making it quite easy to complete.

This principle is behind the beauty of procrastination and why so many people do it. When you procrastinate, you are shrinking the amount of time you are willing to give to a certain task. Consequently, the workload of the task shrinks, making the task easier to do.

In the gas analogy, you are putting the same amount of gas (your desired outcome) into a smaller container (your work time). By doing this, you drop all of the wasted mental energy worrying and get down to the nitty-gritty of just DOING the work. When you procrastinate, you also force yourself to work with 100% energy, doing mental sprints to complete the work on time.

While I have great respect for procrastination, most people procrastinate unconsciously and waste a lot of mental energy being stressed and nervous about their impending deadlines as a result. Even though they work with much greater efficacy when they eventually work, they don't seem to really enjoy the free time they created. Furthermore, after learning about the importance of spaced repetition in encoding memories, procrastinating (the way it's normally done) is very inefficient because you never really get to strengthen the memory networks you spent all that time building.

What I want to teach you to do is how to apply Parkinson's Law in order to harness all of the benefits of procrastination without all of the downsides.

By defining your goals in section I, you got clear about what is important to you and what you want to spend your time doing. Hopefully you reconnected with your passions and interests outside of medicine as well and realized that you aren't willing to devote your entire life to medical school. This awareness will help you to draw a mental boundary of how much time you're willing to give to studying to get the results you want both in medical school and your life in general.

What if you told yourself that you have a maximum of 3 hours a day to get all your studying and learning done for medical school? By doing this, you change the rules of the game, turning the time available for completion of medical school from roughly 12-16 hours/day to 1-3 hours/day.

Using Parkinson's law, the burden of the workload will consequently decrease in proportion to the time you allotted to complete it. This will harness the mental power and focus that procrastination brings, but leaves out the added stress because it is a CONSCIOUS CHOICE. All of a sudden, learning efficiently and effectively becomes VERY important, and this sense of importance will be like mental rocket fuel to your study sessions.

Another way to apply Parkinson's Law is to SCHEDULE fun activities between your planned study sessions. This creates a firm time boundary that encourages you to complete your study sessions before that scheduled activity. For example, if you plan to go surfing with your friend at 1PM, that means that you really need to have get your 1-3 study sessions in before that. Knowing you have this deadline, and the positive emotions of looking forward to it, will give you an extra mental boost to help you work at 100% power when you are studying.

Remember, it's far better to study a few study blocks a day than to save them all up for the week before the test. The more you repeat and actively recall the information on your cards, the better they will be sealed in your long-term memory. In fact, as you do this, you'll find that you hardly have to study for tests. While your friends are stressing out and pulling all-nighters, you'll be studying a few super high yield review flashcards and enjoying your weekend, doing whatever you want.

Once you get used to this system, you'll be amazed at how little you actually have to study, because you're studying in perfect synchrony with your brain. At my school, I watched my colleagues spend 8 hours a day in class, and at least 3-5 hours after class studying and reviewing, for a total of a 11-13 hour work day not counting transportation between locations! After I learned these study methods and put them into practice, my "work day" in the first 2 years of medical school usually consisted of only one or two study blocks, 90 minutes each. I want you to be able to do the same!

Chapter 21: Planning Your Week

Now that you know how long to study at a time, you might also be wondering how many study sessions you'll need to have each day to learn all the material you want. As you slowly abandon the schedule and curriculum your school has given you in lieu of your own custom-designed curriculum, you'll want to get good at pacing yourself and creating a rough schedule for how much you'll need to get done each day or week to meet the learning goals you set for yourself in section I.

After a few weeks, you'll schedule yourself intuitively without thinking about it, but as you start, it's helpful to create a more defined schedule for yourself to ensure you're finishing everything you want to get done. In the process section below, I'll cover just how to get a rough idea of how many study sessions you'll need so that you can plan your schedule accordingly.

By doing this, you're not only ensuring that you'll meet your goals, but you're also eliminating the HUGE burden of stress that most med students feel daily. Most students feel in a perpetual state of being overwhelmed and stressed because they haven't clearly DEFINED the end-points of their studying process.

Instead, you're going to know exactly what you are going to do, and know that you've thoroughly planned a system to get it all done effectively and efficiently. You'll be able to finish your 3-hour study day and then spend the rest of the day at the beach—all the while feeling great knowing that you've completed what you set out to do. You'll soon discover that when you are able to study without stress, you exponentially increase your results.

Process: Making Your Custom Schedule

Now that you've practiced a typical "study day" with blocks of "study sessions" (highly focused mental sprints), interspersed with short and long breaks, in this section we'll figure out just how many blocks you'll want to plan each week in order to meet both your life goals and your academic goals within medical school.

Step 1: Envisioning Your Perfect Study Day

To get started, let's revisit your life goals and medical school goals that you created in section I. As you reread these goals, try to visualize in as much detail as possible what an ideal workday in medical school might look like.

Set aside 20-30 minutes to do some stream of consciousness writing on this. Start your day from when and how you wake up to when and how you go to bed, and get creative about different scenarios that meet most (if not all) of your personal goals.

Try to imagine and visualize days where you study in ranges from 1.5 to 7.5 hours. What will you do with the rest of your free time?

By the end of this step, I want you to feel energized and excited about your life and goals outside of medical school and to feel motivated to not spend your whole day studying. Remember this vision and this feeling as you move on.

Step 2: Figuring Out Your Study Pace

Start by doing a basic study session (i.e. 60-120 minutes), without paying attention to how much you get done. Just focus on making and studying the flashcards at a pace that works for you. When you finish, look back and see how much you got done. Rather than think in terms of lectures or chapters, think in terms of how many pages you got through. Use this information to calculate your own personal pages per hour score.

For example, if you studied 15 pages in 90 minutes, that would be 10 pages/hour (15 pages divided by 1.5 hours). Do this a few more times as you study with various sources.

For example, your pages per hour speed using a high yield source like First Aid will likely be a lot slower than your speed when doing lecture notes. Obviously your speed will differ slightly, but the point of this is to get a rough idea of your pace with different sources.

Step 3: Calculating Your Amount of Study Sessions

You already know from section II the amount of material you want to cover (i.e. The MSK chapter of First Aid, and all the lectures from Dr. Jones, etc....). Remember, you can always add more material, so for this purpose, we're using the amount of study material that, if totally memorized, would meet YOUR academic goals.

Next, group your study material by density. For example it might take you 1 hour to memorize 5 pages of first aid, but you could memorize 30 pages of Dr. Jones' lecture notes in 1 hour.

Now simply figure out roughly how many pages you have to get through in each category, and divide that by your study speed (pages per hour) to get the amount of hours you'll need to study. In the example above, let's say the MSK chapter of First Aid is 25 pages, so at 5 pages per hour, that would take you 5 hours of studying. Then let's say you have 120 pages of notes from Dr. Jones, and at 30 pages per hour, that would be 4 hours. So your total study time in this example would be 9 hours. Now divide that (number of hours) by your typical study session length (i.e. probably 60-120 minutes). The result is the amount of study sessions you'll need to get through your material, not counting the final review.

Step 4: Calculating Your Blocks Per Week

Most of your blocks or sections in medical school will be a minimum of 4 weeks, and a maximum of 6 months. The relative length will help you determine how much time you'll want to leave for review.

A good way to estimate this at first is to refer to your planned schedule, and see which day your final lecture ends. Often this will be the week before the test, and the test-week will consist of review lectures. Using this as a guide, plan to schedule your main study sessions within those learning weeks (don't count the review week/test week). For example, if you were in the Cardiology block, which is 8 weeks long, with the final week being for review and testing, you'd have 7 weeks to schedule your study sessions. If from Step 3, you figured out that for the Cardiology block you would need about 140 study sessions, then divide that by the number of study weeks (140/7), and you'd arrive at 20 sessions per week. Most often, your weekly schedule is going to differ based on your plans for that week, and I don't recommend planning more than one week in advance.

Step 5: Scheduling Your Weeks

Using the example above, you know you want to find a way to fit in 20 study sessions this week. If you chose to study every day, that would be about 3 sessions per day.

You know this is your rough goal, but you have a lot of leeway to customize each day how you want.

For example, if something fun came up, and you only got to 1 or 2 study sessions on Monday, you know you want to add one to a day later in the week. As you think about your weekly schedule, remember Parkinson's Law, and remember the brainstorm and visualization of your perfect day you did in Step 1. As you make your schedule, add your study sessions, but ALSO add the fun activities you want to do to meet your overall life goals. Maybe you want to go on a long weekend trip to Mexico for 4 days to practice surfing. Can you plan to do 2 study sessions on the plane/airport there and back? How about committing to one study session in the afternoon between each surf session? That will give you 8 study sessions during the trip. Then you know you'll have to work hard the other 3 days, averaging 4 study sessions each day in order to meet your weekly goal. As you use Parkinson's Law and schedule your fun activities, this will not only help you to study more efficiently when you do study, but will also give you a boost of positive emotion as you get excited for your weekly plans!

After doing these steps for just 1 study block, you'll start to get an intuitive feel for how much you need to study to meet your goals, and you won't even need to make a schedule for yourself. For now, don't worry about your schedule and process for that last review week before the test, I'll cover that later in the next section.

Chapter 22: Feeding and Watering the Study Machine

Even though the brain makes up only 2% of our body weight, it consumes 20% of the body's energy supply. It consumes more energy per unit size than any muscle in the human body, even more than Arnold's biceps! Because of this incredible metabolic demand, we can only use a small fraction of our brain's capacity at any given time to avoid an energetic blackout of our entire body.

This section will cover the ingredients you need to keep your learning machine functioning at top shape.

Brain Food

Have you ever noticed that after eating a heavy meal (red meat, creams, butters, fast food), you felt great right while tasting it, but then felt very physically and mentally tired about 20 minutes afterwards, maybe even needing a nap? This is no coincidence. To make things simple, large meals, through physical distention of the stomach stimulate gastrin release, and fatty meals stimulate the release of cholecystokinin, which keeps food in your stomach longer, causing even more gastrin release.

Gastrin stimulates parietal cells in your stomach to make more hydrochloric acid from carbon dioxide. The byproduct of this conversion is bicarbonate, and as levels of bicarbonate go up in the blood, our pH increases, creating a temporary metabolic alkalosis. This is called the "Alkaline Tide." The alkalosis then triggers chemoreceptors in our brain to decrease our baseline breathing rate, which in turn decreases the amount of oxygen in our blood and brains, which in turn makes us sleepy and tired until the food has moved out of our stomach. That's a mouthful to remember! The takeaway point is that the larger and more fatty the

meal (the longer your stomach needs to secrete HCl),
the more tired you'll be afterwards, and the less oxygen
you'll have to power your brain for learning.

But wait, there's more! Now think about the last time
you ate a meal with lots of simple carbs, such as a bagel
with butter and jam. What happened? More than
likely, you noticed a pleasurable feeling of satiety, and
even increased energy for about 30 minutes. This was
likely followed by a period of mild irritability and
fatigue, followed by even more hunger.

When the human physiological systems first evolved
during the Paleolithic era, they were "designed" to
process the types of food found in nature at that time
(i.e. nuts, fruits, veggies, meats). These foods have
complex carbohydrates that break down slowly in our
GI tract, releasing a slow and steady level of glucose
into our bloodstream. Our main metabolic hormones,
insulin and glucagon, are designed to work in sync with
these type of naturally occurring complex
carbohydrates.

Unfortunately, evolution takes a long time to happen,
and our bodies haven't yet adapted to the modern diet
of high fructose corn syrup and white bread. These
simple carbohydrates are VERY RAPIDLY turned into
glucose and enter the bloodstream, TRICKING the
pancreas to secrete a HUGE AMOUNT of insulin. And
if that wasn't enough, they also stimulate the small
intestine to secrete gastric inhibitory polypeptide,
which potentiates the secretion of Insulin in response to
glucose, in essence giving a TURBO BOOST of insulin
in addition to the amount already released. The huge
problem here is that with these manmade simple carbs,
there is NO steady stream of Glucose consistently
entering the bloodstream, but the HUGE AMOUNT of
Insulin (with a half-life designed to match digestion of
complex carbs) has already been released. After the

initial bolus of glucose has been stored (making us fat), there is still A LOT of excess insulin in our blood, which brings our bodies into a temporary state of HYPOglycemia. This then triggers the release of Epinephrine (adrenaline), and Glucagon, which makes us feel anxious, irritable, tired, and eventually just as hungry as when we started. NOT a fun cycle to be in if you are studying.

Next time you're in the library take a look around and see what students are eating and snacking on. Most often you'll see fast food, candy, pastries, and other HIGH SUGAR, HIGH FAT foods! In short, the two worst possible ingredients you could be feeding your body if your goal is to learn efficiently. Don't get me wrong, I have nothing against some tasty pizza every now and then, but just don't do it right before or during a study session.

Using the same logic above, your ideal study meal would be SMALL, high in proteins and complex carbs (i.e. vegetables) and relatively low in fat. To help you choose foods that your body knows how to process, try "the great grandma test." Michael Pollan, author of the bestselling book The Omnivore's Dilemma[7], offers this simple test to help you decide what to eat. Before you eat something, take a look at what you're about to eat and ask yourself if your great grandma would recognize it as food (i.e. no EZ Mac, no otter pops, no Top Ramen). But if great grandma would think it's food and would eat it (i.e. eggs, veggies, meat, beans, fruits), then your body's physiology would probably agree with it too.

Here are some of my favorites:

---

[7] Pollan, M. (2006). The omnivore's dilemma: A natural history of four meals. New York: Penguin Press.

Breakfast:
- Steel-cut oats, yogurt, or cottage cheese with raw walnuts and blueberries
- Eggs: hard-boiled or scrambled with veggies
- Fruit smoothies with added protein powder

Lunch and Dinner:
- Salad with protein (chicken, avocado, eggs, nuts etc....)
- Chicken or Tofu and steamed veggies.

Snacks:
- Raw Nuts (almonds, walnuts, cashews)
- Avocado slices with lime juice and salt
- Edamame
- Fresh or dried fruit.

Brain Drinks

Again—take a look around the library, how many Monsters, Red Bulls, sodas, and orange mocha frappuccinos do you see?

Caffeine and sugar actually can be helpful, but in moderation, and only when you use them correctly... let's go over these.

Caffeine

Caffeine is a bit of a double-edged sword. When used properly in moderation, it can enhance memory and learning, can improve your mood, and can make studying more enjoyable. If you use too much however, it actually has a negative effect on learning and memory by creating chronic stress and anxiety and disrupting your daily sleep cycle. So our goal is to use caffeine in the best way possible for our brains.

Caffeine has been shown in many studies to be beneficial in both short and long-term memory. This is no surprise. However, the studies suggest that this effect on memory is only seen in habitual drinkers, and is seen when the caffeine is taken while learning, and after learning, but NOT before learning (i.e. the morning cup of coffee doesn't help you during your afternoon study session). Furthermore, the best results were seen with a mean weekly ingestion of about 700 milligrams, or 100 mg/day. A tall Starbucks has about 150mg, a venti has 450mg, and a monster has about 160mg. In contrast, green tea has about 30mg/glass, and black tea 50mg/glass. Also, this amount will vary GREATLY from person to person. This is due to our tolerance, body size, and our genetic polymorphisms of the CYP450 1A2 subtype.

Furthermore, it's useful to know that caffeine reaches peak plasma levels (and peak effects) in 50-60 minutes. Obviously, the higher the dose, the stronger the effects AND the stronger the withdrawal symptoms (i.e. headache, fatigue, irritability) after peak plasma levels. Therefore, for our purposes, you want to avoid HIGH dose caffeine beverages most of the time. The only time you'd want to use this is if you want higher performance for a short period of time (less than 60 minutes), and are willing to go through the unpleasant effects of the withdrawal (similar to akathisia) after that period. An example of when you might do this is about 1 hour before the end of the last study session of your day, or during the last hour of a test.

Knowing this, consistently drinking coffee throughout the day is usually counterproductive because of the high concentration of caffeine and subsequent withdrawal effects. However, you could have 4-5 glasses of green tea in a day while studying without a problem because of its lower concentration of caffeine.

Personally, my favorite thing to do is to have a cup of coffee with lots of skim milk during my first study session, and then slowly sip tea for the remaining study sessions. This is the pharmacological equivalent of a loading dose, then maintenance dose.

BOTTOM LINE--it's best to use caffeine daily in low doses, and the best TIME to use caffeine is during and after your study sessions, not before (i.e. no morning cup of coffee).

Sugar (Glucose)

Glucose is a type of sugar, and is the main energy source for our brain and the rest of our body. Most of the foods we eat are converted to glucose at some point for us to use as fuel to make energy in the form of ATP. A steady supply of glucose is integral for the process of long term potentiation, forming memories, and learning.

Like I mentioned above, our bodies know how to convert natural foods into a steady supply of glucose for our brain. However when we eat high quantities of simple carbs (which are rare in nature) such as high fructose corn syrup, white bread, pasta, or rice, our bodies aren't equipped to handle this and it throws our metabolic system into haywire causing a short-term sugar high followed by a crash about 30 minutes later (the half-life of insulin is about 5 minutes, so 5 half lives is about 25 minutes).

Simple sugar is bad news if you are trying to study. Try to eliminate simple sugar all together when you study but if you must have it, have it in very low doses and in a steady concentration (i.e. a small bit of honey in your cup of green tea).

A much better way to give your brain a steady supply of glucose is with foods that pass the "great grandma test" I described earlier. This give your brain the steady supply of glucose it needs to power learning without all the adverse effects of the hormonal cascade caused by consuming simple carbs and pure sugar.

What about Splenda?

There are two things about non-sugar sweeteners that I don't like. The first is that all of them are chemically different when they are excreted from our bodies, and we don't yet understand how they are processed in the body. They come in one way; they come out another way, but what happened in between?

The second problem is that the taste of sweetness alone (regardless of the presence of glucose) is thought to trigger GLP-1 and potentiate insulin release through a hormone called gustducin.

So in this case we release insulin but because these are fake sugars, we never actually get a real glucose load, and the result is a hormonal cascade that causes the same irritability and fatigue that happens after eating simple sugars.

The best solution is to avoid these artificial sweeteners too, and re-train yourself to get used to things being not so sweet (this will take about 4-6 weeks to get used to). However, if you love that sweet taste, things like Splenda are probably fine and definitely better than pure sugar for the purpose of efficient learning.

Water

You'll be amazed at just how much energy drinking water will give you.

The majority of us are chronically mildly dehydrated, drinking far less than the recommended 8 cups of water a day. As you start to drink water regularly, even when you're not thirsty, you'll likely feel better, have fewer headaches, and have a lot more energy.

A simple way to accomplish this is to always be in the habit of drinking something while you're studying. As I talked about earlier, things like iced green tea are the perfect study drink because they have a lot of water combined with low-dose caffeine. Or if you prefer a small amount of coffee, have a large glass of water after it.

Brain Supplements

As you learned in section 3, learning new material is a highly complex process that involves not only changes in the electrochemical milieu of your brain but also changes in your neuroanatomy! When you are doing the type of mental sprints described in this section, you are using your brain like a racecar in full throttle.

In addition to resting it and having breaks, you can assist your brain in learning by making sure it has the right types of fuel and maintenance to keep this pace up. Most of these fuels can be found in quality and types of foods you eat before and while learning, which we covered in the last section. Here, I'll go into some key supplements you might want to consider taking to give your brain ample supply of everything it needs for learning.

B Complex

These are the basic brain vitamins. If you look at the labels, you'll notice that these are in all of the energy drinks and supplements. Lets take a look at the ones relevant to optimal learning.

- **Vitamin B3:** Niacin is one of the key ingredients in the co-enzymes NAD, and NADP, which if you haven't learned already, are involved in over 200 enzymes in the body! The most relevant to our discussion is its role in producing ATP, the primary energy source of the body (and brain).

- **Vitamin B6:** This vitamin is a cofactor in several important enzymes including pyridoxal 5'-phosphate (PLP). In the central nervous system, this enzyme is involved in the synthesis of most neurotransmitters, including dopamine, serotonin, GABA, and norepinephrine. PLP is also abundant in muscle tissue, where it assists in the reaction of turning glycogen into glucose. Because dopamine is the key neurotransmitter linked to attention and memory, and because of the brains HUGE demand for a steady diet of glucose, this is a key brain vitamin. This is also one of the few vitamins that can be toxic in overdose, so keep your daily dose under 50mg to avoid possible neuropathy. Most B-Complex formulations have FAR less than this, so it shouldn't be a problem.

- **Vitamin B12:** The main functions of Vitamin B12 are to create energy from fats and proteins using the enzyme methylmalonyl-CoA mutase, and to create the primary methyl donor molecule, methionine using the enzyme methionine synthase. The latter reaction is used to create S-Adenosyl methionine, the body's main methyl donor group, which is involved in the synthesis of MANY proteins, including neurotransmitters. It is also thought to enhance the action of both serotonin and dopamine in the brain. Again, we see Vitamin B12 important in the role of energy and dopamine, both key ingredients to efficient learning. However, not all vitamin B12s are created equal! Vitamin B12 actually refers to a CLASS of similar chemical compounds called "cobalamins." Most oral supplements contain an artificial form called "cyanocobalamin" while most intramuscular injections are in an artificial form called hydroxycobalamin, both of which are thought to be storage forms of the vitamin. In the liver, cyanocobalamin is then converted to hydroxycobalamin, which is then eventually converted to the 2 active forms, methylcobalamin (used in the enzyme methionine synthase) and 5-deoxyadenosyl cobalamin (used in the enzyme methylmalonyl-CoA mutase). 7 different intracellular enzymes (Cb1 A all the way to Cb1 G) are involved in preparing the active forms of these vitamins, and as we learned when looking at caffeine, people vary greatly (genetic polymorphisms) in the speed of these enzymes. Therefore, to hedge your bets, regardless of your own enzyme speed, I recommend buying vitamins that have B12 in its active form (methylcobalamin and 5-adenosylcobalamin) when possible.

- **Folic Acid:** Folic acid, AKA vitamin B9, is also used in a variety of biochemical reasons including making DNA and RNA for new cells, amino acid metabolism to create new proteins, and in the creation of the methyl-donor molecule S-Adenosyl methionine, mentioned earlier. As we learn, we are not only creating new neural connections and networks, but are actually building new neurons as well, and folic acid is essential in that process. Like vitamin B12, folic acid also comes in a variety of forms. Folic acid, the inactive form, is converted in the liver (through 4 reactions) to it's active form L-5-methyltetrahydrofolate, also known as folinic acid, which is the form of the vitamin used to carry out it's important functions in learning. Also, as is the case with Vitamin B12, a variety of factors including genetic polymorphisms can alter the production of folinic acid from folic acid, and therefore, your best bet is to take folinic acid directly. In fact, this active form of folic acid is so powerful in assisting the brain to create key neurotransmitters, that it's used as a prescription drug to augment the treatment of Major Depression (Deplin).

- A typical B-Complex supplement will contain all of these essential vitamins. However, if possible, look for ones that contain the active form of the vitamins. Here's a review of the active forms:
    - B3: Look for a supplement with about 75% Niacinamide and 25% Niacin
    - B6: The active form you want is Pyridoxine Hydrochloride
    - B12: Look for about 50% as methylcobalamin and 50% as 5-adenosylcobalamin
    - Folic Acid: Look for folinic acid, or L-5-methyltetrahydrofolate

Phosphatidylserine

Phosphatidylserine is the most abundant phospholipid in the human brain. It is a key component in the phospholipid bilayer of neurons and essential for membrane integrity and neuronal function. When you make new memory networks, you are actually building new neurons and new neuronal connections, so having this phospholipid already in the area is like having a million construction workers poised and handing memory bricks to your brain as it makes new memory networks.

Phosphatidylserine has also been documented to help increase the availability of choline, which is used to make Acetylcholine, a key neurotransmitter involved in learning and memory.

Phosphatidylserine is thought to be quite safe and is recognized by the FDA as "Generally Recognized as Safe" in doses of up to 200mg three times a day. I would generally take this during the final review phase of studying (the week before the test), and usually take 100mg before each study session, with a maximum of 300mg per day.

L-Theanine

This is a unique amino acid found almost exclusively in green tea. It has some remarkable effects on the brain and is thought to simultaneously increase GABA and Dopamine levels while promoting alpha wave activity from thalamic pacemaker cells (EEG waves produced during states of wakeful relaxation). The result is a state of calm yet focused alertness that is found to work synergistically with caffeine. It is also categorized by the FDA as "Generally Recognized as Safe" in food and beverages in doses of up to 250mg per serving. A cup of green tea is thought to have approximately 5mg and you can get many of these beneficial effects from drinking green tea alone. I would often take 100mg with my first cup of coffee before my first morning study session. Remember, if you do take this as a supplement, to take it with caffeine, because it will work synergistically.

Chapter 23: Putting it All Together—The Sample Study Session

We just covered a lot of material, and you're likely overwhelmed by it all. In this short section, I'll go through an ideal study day to see what it might look like when you apply all of these learning principles together.

7:00 AM: Starting the Day

You wake up naturally to the sunlight coming through the window of the Beach Hut you and your best friend are staying at in Kauai (You noticed that there were no mandatory classes this week, so you signed up for a credit card and used the mileage bonus to book a free flight out there).

Because your mind is usually freshest in the morning, you guys decide to study in the morning and then plan to surf after lunch (applying Parkinson's Law by scheduling a fun activity after studying, thereby decreasing the amount of time you have to study and harnessing the power of procrastination to work more efficiently).

7:30 – 9:30 AM: First Study Session

After a healthy breakfast (scrambled eggs with veggies) and taking your B-Complex, you head to an awesome local coffee shop, order your favorite coffee (your caffeine loading dose), and use it to wash down your 100mg L-Theanine and 100mg of Phosphatidylserine.

You and your buddy set up at a table outside with your laptop and a pad of legal paper to write down your answers to your flashcard questions.

You turn your phone on airplane mode, close down your email program, put on your headphones and fire up some techno music, set a timer for 90 minutes on your phone to tell you to stop, and then get started with your electronic flashcards.

About 20 minutes in, you notice that there is a concept that just doesn't make sense and hasn't been answered by the other material in your review book—you open up your Evernote or Word Document you use to track these kinds of things and add it to your list of questions (later that week you'll email your professor with those questions if they haven't been answered already).

Back to the cards. After finishing the first round and reviewing them, you are amazed at how much you have remembered after just one run-through. You start feeling really good—excited about being in Kauai, smelling the pungent plumeria growing in the garden near your outdoor table, learning really cool things about the human body, and excited about the great surf session you're going to have later. Life is good.

9:30 AM – 10:00 AM: Break-Time

Your timer lets you know your done, good work! You check the surf report and see that the tide is going to be perfect at 1:00 PM, giving you further motivation to get another high quality study session in before heading out. You reload with a lower dose caffeine beverage like green tea, and snack on some raw walnuts and a handful of blueberries while having a great conversation with your best friend, or checking your phone, email, social media, etc....

10:00 AM – 11:30 AM: Second Study Session

Break's over. Time to get back to work. You shut down your email, put your phone back in airplane mode, start your music back up, and set another timer for 90 minutes. You get back into a state of "flow" while studying using 100% mental power. By now, some of the material you're studying is review for you, and you're connecting the dots in the material between totally different subjects.

Feeling great about yourself, your rapid learning, and your plans for the rest of your day, time flies, and in what seems like 15 minutes, your alarm is buzzing telling you to stop studying.

11:30 AM – Midnight: Continue to Have a Great Day

You grab a quick healthy lunch before you and your buddy paddle out. Of course, the surf is epic, and you feel great knowing that you've put in some solid work.

You have the rest of the day to pursue your broader life goals, whether that's exercise to create a healthy body, building important relationships, learning guitar, whatever you're excited about!

Or perhaps you wanted to get in 3 or 4 total study sessions today. In that case, after surfing (your long break involving exercise and something fun), you head to a different coffee shop or back to your beach cottage (remember the importance of keeping things new), and repeat the above for 1 or 2 more sessions. In the worst case scenario (4 study sessions), you'll still be done around 6pm and have the rest of the day and night to do whatever you want.

While this day is simplified, the basic structure is totally realistic and what most of my study days looked like after I started using these techniques (granted, I wasn't always in Kauai but I was spending most of my time in beautiful places I loved). Most days I'd study 1-2 90 minute sessions, other days like the week before the test, I'd do 3-4 sessions. But even then, I really had a good time during the process of studying and I still had PLENTY of free time to enjoy my life outside of school. I want the same for you. I want you to have the life of your dreams NOW AND in the future!

Lets review. In this section, you learned the nitty gritty details of putting the study system you learned in section III into practice. We started by reviewing how to efficiently find and seal the gaps in your knowledge in order to create a comprehensive and seamless memory network. We then looked at the question of where to study—learning the importance of choosing places that are both fun (even if they're loud), and new to us. Once at our study location, we reviewed how to set up our workspace by minimizing our distractions and experimenting with studying while listening to music. We then went over the concept of a study session, an intense focused burst of mental activity for a defined amount of time. You learned to set time-based goals rather than subject-based goals and figured out your own mental range (usually 60-120 minutes) for your ideal study session. You learned about the importance of scheduled breaks between sessions and discovered activities that revitalize and refresh you during those breaks. You then calculated how many study sessions you'll need to accomplish your academic goals and added those study sessions to your daily and weekly schedule. As you did this, you were sure to use Parkinson's Law to schedule planned fun activities after your study sessions to motivate and energize you while you study. Finally, you learned about how to fuel the study machine, and reviewed important concepts to keep in mind when choosing what types of foods, drinks, and supplements you put in your body.

As you get used to the basic study system from section III, and add in the finer points you learned in this section, your study process will become even more seamless and efficient. All that is left now is to practice, practice, practice! The more you practice these techniques, the more natural and habitual they will become, and within 6 weeks, you'll be able to do all of these principles without even thinking about them.

All that's left is covering the details of how to best review for and take tests, which will cover in the next and final section ...

Section V: Testing—The Final Review and What to Do on Test Day

You've already constructed an amazing virtual memory skyscraper. This final review phase is about learning your way around the place, being comfortable moving from room to room, taking the elevator to different floors, and knowing where the fire escapes are.

You've spent a lot of time studying and learning your chosen material efficiently yet effectively. You have carefully and thoroughly built your memory networks, which is the most time and energy intensive part of the learning process. This final review phase is what is required to complete your memory skyscraper so that you can actually USE it when your trying to recall the information for exams and while seeing patients or doing research.

By the end of this section, you will know exactly how to review the flashcards you've already made and learned in an efficient and productive way. And, instead or constantly worrying that there could be more you could study before you're exam, you'll have a defined end-point of when your review phase is done, so that you can relax and do whatever you want before the test.

Like a marathon racer in the last few days before the race, you've already done the hard work, the training is complete. All that's left is to have fun and show off your skills as you run the mental race of your exam.

In this section we will also go over top test-taking strategies, and you will know how to apply and use these on the exam itself so that you can easily recall the information you've worked so hard to learn. You will also learn how to master the inner mental game of test-taking itself so that you can be sure that the testing environment doesn't block you from being able to remember everything you just learned.

In fact you may discover that you actually enjoy reviewing for tests and the test itself! As I mentioned in section III, organizational psychologist Mihaly Csikszentmihalyi wrote a best-selling book called "Flow[8]," in which he describes a state of being where people feel incredibly fulfilled and aren't even aware of time passing. In his studies, people describe this state as one of the best parts of their day, they feel exhilarated and alive. In his research for the types of situations where most people feel this state of flow, he discovered something extraordinary—that people were most often in this heightened state of "flow" while at work! Most people, by default think of work as a drag, as something they "have to" do. However, when you get to be really good at something and perfect it and are able to focus on that single task, people often experience a state of flow!

As medical students, our "work" is the work of studying and learning. For many people, it's a drag because it seems like we'll never get done, that there is just too much to learn, or that we're not making any progress. However, through the study and review methods you're practicing in this book, you're learning to overcome these obstacles--choosing a do-able amount of work, with a clear endpoint of when your studying is done. When you study this way, most students experience this state of "flow" during the review phase and during tests itself. It is my sincere hope that this will be true for you too, and that you'll actually look forward to test day, as a fun time to show off your knowledge and skills!

---

[8] Csikszentmihalyi, M. (1990). *Flow: The psychology of optimal experience*. New York: Harper & Row.

Chapter 24: The Targeted Review

Ideally, by the time you arrive at the review phase, you have completed the steps described in the previous sections, especially section III. Specifically, before reading on, ensure that:

- You tested your immediate memory right after writing your own personalized question to each flash card.

- You then tested your short-term memory of the information after finishing your first block of 5-8 cards, re-testing yourself on this "deck" of cards until you were able to recall the answers on EACH of the cards.

- After finishing the whole "deck" (usually 15-50 flashcards) representing a book chapter, a lecture, or however else you chose to divide up your information, you tested your longer-term memory by studying blocks of "shuffled" cards, usually 5-8 cards at a time, until you were able to recall the answers on EACH of the cards.

- "Flagging" the cards you didn't get the 1st time around from this last step, and moving them to a separate "deck" called something like "Flagged Cards."

- You finished doing this for all your information (i.e. the whole chapter, or all your lecture notes, etc....) and you have about 3-5 days left depending on how you scheduled your review time (from section 4).

By doing these steps, you've seen and ACTIVLEY RECALLED the information on each card about 5-10 times, depending on how many times you needed to review each card before moving on. As I mentioned above, this is the bulk of your learning, and the information is quite well sealed in your memory networks.

Our focus in this final review phase of learning is going to be solely on the cards you "flagged." You can rest assured that the cards you didn't flag, the ones you were able to independently recall the first-time around even after they were shuffled, are memorized.

The information represented by the "flagged" cards will be different for each student, and they represent a SMALL but VERY HIGH YIELD body of information that is ideal to use for review. AND they are in question/answer format, which will be just like your test!

Our next steps will be to move these cards into a new "deck," then "un-flag" them, and re-study them in shuffled blocks, "re-flagging" the ones you didn't get on the first try, and repeating this process (which will be faster and faster) until you eventually are able to recall all your cards on the first try.

Most students find this phase of studying to be very rewarding and even fun because you are constantly positively reinforced by how well you know the details of what you've already studied. Furthermore, you'll likely find that you will easily get into a state of "Flow" during your review study sessions. Let's get started!

Process: The Targeted Review

What follows is a step-by-step description of how to review and organize your flagged cards, and just like in section III, you can find videos on the website (www.facebook.com/studycoachmd) showing you how to do this. In the following instructions, I show you exactly what I do on a Mac computer using the iFlash program however the basic commands and idea of what I talk about is easily applicable to the PC and Anki or other flashcard programs you may prefer.

1. Open up a new flashcard deck for review (I call this deck "keepers"). Then open up all your other decks,

select the flagged cards (Use Command + Mouse Click to select individual cards), and drag the flagged cards to your new deck. By the end of this process, your new deck will have only flagged cards, drawn from each of the other decks you created previously.

2. Now that all the flagged cards are in your test review deck, "un-flag" the cards (Shift +Command + K) to reset this deck so that you can "re-flag" the ones you still don't know.

3. Study these high yield cards in groups of 5-8 cards at a time, shuffled, in the same way you studied the cards in section III. Again—if you don't know the information on the 1st go-around, "re-flag" the card.

4. Move the newly re-flagged cards into another deck, called something like "Level 1 Keepers", then un-flag them, and repeat step 3, each time making a higher level of keepers (i.e. Level 2, Level 3, etc....).

5. Continue this process until you have no more flagged cards.

*** *Remember to use all the details about effective study sessions from* section *IV as you are doing these steps!*

It's that simple! Also, as you're doing this, I recommend that during your exercise sessions or in your car, that you listen to audio reviews of the information if you have them. Not only does hearing the material strengthen your memory network, but it will also help you connect the dots in a different way. You'll notice that by listening to audio reviews now (after you've reviewed and mastered the material), you'll be able to pick up on small valuable details you missed the first time around.

Chapter 25: Mastering Effective Test-Taking Strategies

Just like there are strategies for learning and encoding information into your mind, there are effective strategies for taking practice tests. Below is a list of basic strategies that have been tested and proven with many students to be effective. For now just think about each of them, and then you'll have a chance to practice them in the next step of this section.

The Mind Dump

The mind dump is used to store a small amount of useful yet difficult-to-memorize information for test day. Information like chromosome numbers, genetics equations, HLA-associations, etc.... in which you don't really know the "why" of, so it isn't connected to other memory networks and you are at risk of forgetting very quickly.

For this type of information, I recommend making a very short review sheet, which you'll read over and over again before walking into your test, then throw it away, and keep repeating the info in your head until the test proctor allows you to write on scratch paper. At this point you'll take a "mind-dump" and transfer all this information you've been keeping in your working memory onto paper, so that you can reference it later when you need it. By the end of the mind dump, your brain should feel clear so that you can focus on the questions in front of you.

Pace Yourself

Look at how many questions you have and how much time you have, and then jot down on your scratch paper about what time you should be halfway.

For example, if you're doing a typical 46 question USMLE block, you have 60 minutes to complete it, so on your paper you'd mark that after 30 minutes, you should be on question 23. When your taking the test and you get to this half-way point, you'll have an idea (based on how much time you've already spent) of how fast you need to go for the 2nd half of the test.

Prioritize Your Questions

For most tests, this won't be an issue, as you'll have plenty of time. But if it's a very time-intensive test where you likely won't finish all the questions (i.e. a 3rd year shelf exam), then you may want to take the test in a different order, depending on how the test is structured.

For example, in the 3rd year shelf exams, the last group of questions often have lots of choices (i.e. A-K), whereas the other questions usually have only 4 choices (A-D). So, if you run out of time and have to end up guessing on the last test questions, you have a better chance guessing right on the 4-choice questions (25%), than on the 11-choice questions (9%). In this case, you'd want to START with the LAST 10 questions of the test, and then go back to the beginning of the test.

How to Approach a Test Question

Read the last sentence first: Often, exam questions can be 2-3 paragraphs long, and you can waste a lot of time if you dive into that material without knowing what to focus on.

For example, a question stem might say that an obese patient came in complaining of frequent urination and being thirsty (at this point, you're wondering if he has diabetes), and then goes on in the last paragraph to say, "your diagnostic tests reveal he has Type II Diabetes and you start him on Metformin, what is the most frequent side effect of this treatment?"

In this case, most of the information in the paragraphs above is irrelevant, and you could answer the question by ONLY reading the last sentence. In other cases it won't be this straight-forward, but almost always, reading the last sentence and taking a moment to think about the question before reading the above paragraphs will help you to be efficient while taking the test.

If you're still confused about what the question is after reading the last sentence, glance at the answer choices, which should help you get a clearer idea of what this question is trying to ask.

Notice and Highlight Key Words

When you're reading the last sentence, take note if you see words like: usually, always, never, every, almost, rarely, except, etc....

If you see these kinds of qualifying words, put a big circle around them because they are easy to skim over and they can trick you if you miss them.

For example, "All the following are true about Neurofibromatosis except: ..." If you read option A and you know it's true, you might just pick that instead of choosing the incorrect answer.

Read the First Sentence

Now that you have an idea of what the question is trying to ask, the first sentence will help you narrow down what you want to focus on.

Typically, the first sentence will tell you the basic demographics of your patient, such as their age, gender, chief complaint, and past medical history. It will also tell you the "setting"—Office vs. Emergency Room vs. Hospital will give you a lot of information to narrow your focus as you read the rest of the question.

After reading the last sentence to get the question and the first sentence to understand the basic demographics of the patient in question, take a moment (close your eyes if you have to) to picture the scene, what's going on, and what the problem is you need to solve.

Skim the Rest of the Question

Now with a clear idea of the problem set before you in this test question, you can skim the rest of the question and highlight or circle key words that stick out to you as relevant or important.

Trust yourself as you go—you now have a clear concept of what this question is about and the relevant memory networks have been activated—trust your intuition as you move along and highlight any other information that seems relevant to you. This type of active reading will help you to stay focused.

Choose Your Best Answer

After doing the above steps, by the time you get to the last sentence (with the question stem), you'll likely already know the correct answer even without reading the answer choices. However, still make it a point to at least skim EVERY answer choice. Some questions try to trick you by saying, "choose the best answer" and while choice A or B might be a good answer, choice D could end up being the "best."

You would hate to have chosen choice A and moved on without even realizing choice D existed. After reading all the options, if you are confident in your answer choice, go for it, and move on.

Track the Questions You Aren't Sure About

If you don't think you know the answer, cross out the potential answers you know aren't right (to increase your chances of guessing right), and put a little dash or some other marker by the answers you think MAY be right, and go with your best guess for what you think is most right.

Then mark the question so you can come back to it. If you're on a computerized exam, there is usually a way to put a check mark at that question.

If you're doing a paper exam, I like to have two different levels of marking questions that I'm not sure about. If I feel like I have a pretty good idea of the right answer, but I'm not totally sure, I circle the question. If I have NO idea, or the material is totally foreign to me, I'll put a star by the question. That way, I can prioritize which questions to come back to when I review.

The point of this process is not to spend a lot of time getting hung up on a question you're unsure about...efficiently make your best guess, mark the question to come back to, and move on.

Reviewing Your Answers

After finishing all the questions if you have extra time (you may not and that's ok too), go back to the questions you marked. Many times, by synchronicity, you will get the information you'll need from another question on the test, and you'll now have enough information to know the correct answer. Other times, you'll find you just had a mental block the first time you saw the question, and when you come back to it later, you may be able to think about the question differently.

If you were able to do two different levels of marking (i.e. circle vs. star), then go back to the ones you TOTALLY didn't know first (the starred questions in my example). Studies have shown that for questions students aren't sure about, they're usually right on their first guess, and most students who change answers will change them from the correct to an incorrect answer. However, on the group of questions you had no idea about, it was a wild guess, so hopefully you got some more info from taking the rest of the test to help you think about these in a different way.

After reviewing these, go over the other questions you weren't sure about. If you have new info to choose a better answer, great, change your answer, however if you're still just as unsure, keep your first guess answer, because that odds are that it's more likely to be correct.

Use All of Your Time

There are no benefits to finishing early. You may feel totally bored and want to get out of there as fast as possible, but that extra 5-10 minutes of free time just isn't worth it.

Get in the habit of staying and reviewing your questions until the time is up. Often, after finishing a test, any stress you might have had will be gone because you're done, and without that extra stress, you can think more clearly about questions.

Also, try not to pay attention to the people that leave early. Many other students WILL leave early, and sometimes this can stress out some students, making them think they're behind, or not as smart as that student who left early. The truth is, everyone works at a different pace, and you have NOTHING to lose by taking all your time. Whether you need it or not, I recommend always taking all your time in a test.

Fill in Your Answers in Blocks

Most tests are computerized now, so this isn't really an issue. But if you still take paper tests, rather than enter them one by one on your answer sheet, finish the whole test first, circling the answers, and after you're done reviewing your answers, then enter all the answers on your answer sheet in one process.

This will save you the precious time of going back and forth between your test booklet and answer sheet, and will prevent you from having to erase anything on your answer sheet and risk a mis-read from the automated scoring machine if your school uses those.

Stimulate and Re-Fuel Your Brain

If you are allowed snacks and drinks into the exam, take advantage of this.

Using what you learned in section IV, I recommend having a lightly caffeinated beverage such as green tea to constantly sip on while taking the test, and then a higher-octane drink such as coffee or an energy drink to use for the final 60-90 minutes of your test.

Remember, because of the pharmacodynamics of caffeine, these high-caffeine beverages will give you energy and concentration for a short amount of time until you build to peak levels (about 60-90min), then, kind of like a "caffeine hangover" you'll actually be more irritable and it will be harder to focus.

Also, remember to have healthy brain-snacks to much on throughout the test if you get hungry... things like nuts, fruits, carrot sticks, celery and peanut butter, yogurt or cottage cheese, etc.... Just eat a little bit and eat frequently to avoid the fatigue from alkaline tide.

Chapter 26: Getting Comfortable with the Testing Experience— Practice Tests

When getting ready for a marathon, or any big race for that matter, runners try to mimic the setting of their eventual race as close as possible. If they can, they'll run the same course, using the same shoes and clothes they'll use on race day, and eating the same breakfast they'll eat as well! The more similar they can make their training sessions to the race day, the more prepared they'll be when the big day comes.

In the same way, you want to treat test day like a marathon, and as you train you want to simulate test day as best you can. Practice tests have a huge amount of benefits; here are just some of them:

Habituate Your Strategies

Taking several practice tests will give you an opportunity to practice all of the test-taking strategies that you just learned, and will give you time to customize them so you can develop the strategies that work best for you.

As you get used to doing this in practice tests, they will eventually become second nature to you, and when the real test comes along, you'll naturally use YOUR best strategies without even thinking about them.

Perfecting Your Timing

A lot of the test-taking game is about getting used to answering questions FAST. This is especially true for your third-year clerkship exams, which may feel like the fastest tests you've ever had.

The more practice tests you do under timed conditions, the more ready you'll be for the big day. Once you get used to thinking at this speed, your brain will be habitually paced to the same pace you'll need for your test, and you'll be able to get through the exam in time simply by using your "default" speed.

Sustaining Your Attention

Another purpose of practice tests is getting used to focusing for a long time. While learning your material, you've been studying in short intense bursts of focus. For test day, you'll want to hone the skills of extending your focus for longer chunks of time. This is most relevant with the USMLE exams, where you'll have to learn how to focus for up to 9 hours!

Fortunately, recalling information for tests doesn't take nearly as much mental energy as encoding the information when you learned it. Also, most system tests won't be longer than a single burst you're used to (90-120min), and in longer tests like the USMLE, you can break up your blocks (60 minutes each) with 10-minute breaks, which is very similar to the way you studied when learning the material.

Avoiding Surprises

All sorts of surprises can happen during tests that can throw off your mental game. Sometimes, you might get really interested in a question, thinking that the answer is just on the tip of your tongue but you're not sure, and then before you know it, 10 minutes have gone by and you're still on the same question.

Or, in another instance, you might come across three tough questions in a row that you have no idea how to answer, and you go into a downward spiral of self-doubt that permeates your mind throughout the whole test, getting in the way of your ability to recall the information you actually DO know.

When you do timed practice tests, you get to make all these mistakes and learn how to get past them before the actual test day, so that when the big day comes around, you're prepared because you've seen it all.

Process: How to Take a Practice Test

Fortunately, you're already ahead of the game, because you've been studying flashcards in question-answer format, which is the same style of active learning that tests are designed around. Your mind is already used to thinking in this way, so a formal practice test won't be a big step up from this.

Step 1: Gather Your Material

Depending on what test you're taking, it may be easy or hard to put together a practice test. If you're doing a practice test for the USMLE, it's easy to simulate a 46 question block using USMLE World, or QBank, or the NBME Practice tests that are available online. This is ideal. However, because board questions will be quite similar to your system exam questions, you could also use a service like USMLE World to create a practice test for your system (in preferences, you can choose only questions from "GI" or "Pathology" or "Physiology").

However, if you're not subscribed to any of these services, ask your professors or upper classmen if there are any old tests available that you could use for practice. If that doesn't work, then just use your highest yield flash cards to review (the ones you flagged in the section before).

Step 2: Set Up Your Environment

Just like the marathoner, the more realistic the simulation, the better you'll perform. For most people, it's enough just to take the test under timed conditions, but for others you may want to take the practice test in the same room the real test will be in, using similar paper, or computers, etc.... Experiment with what works best for you and do that.

Step 3: Take the Test

Set up the timer, and go for it. Take out the list of test-taking strategies from the step above and use them!

Step 4: Review the Test

Wait to review the test until you've taken all the test-blocks you plan on taking for that day. For example, if you're doing a system test that will be 2 hours long, you might take 2 practice test blocks (60min each) back to back on USMLE World to simulate the whole 2-hour test.

If you're doing a Step 1 simulation, you might take eight 60-minute blocks back to back with a 10-minute break in between each. Regardless of your situation, wait until you're done with the whole simulated test before reviewing it.

As you review it, for the questions you got right, just skim the answer/explanation to make sure you got it right for the right reason, rather than just guessing. If you didn't, or if you were missing some key information, enter that into some new flashcards in a new deck called something like "Practice Tests."

For questions you got wrong, make sure you know why you got them wrong, and then enter the key relevant information you'd need to get them right into your flashcards. If there are some major conceptual things you just don't get that keep coming up, or if you miss a lot of questions on the same subject, and if the test answer doesn't explain it enough for you to know the "WHY" of your error, then go back to the original source to review those cards again. In extreme cases, you may even want to actually watch that lecture (I recommend double-speed webcast) to really hear it explained.

At first, this review process may take a long time to do, probably twice as long as it took to actually take the test, but it's totally worth it.

By the end of the review process, you should have the relevant information you learned entered into a new deck of flash cards. This material is like gold; it's personally relevant, high yield material that is sealing the cracks in your knowledge base.

Finally, when it comes to practice tests, quality is better than quantity. Your time is much better spent doing 1 or 2 in-depth quality practice tests then doing 6-7 practice tests where you just skim the answers in the review. You know you did a quality review when, after studying these "practice test" flashcards in the same way you'd study any cards, you could re-take the test and get near 100%.

Chapter 27: Mastering the Mental Game of Test Taking

By now you've not only mastered the material for your exam, but you've also mastered the best test taking strategies that work for you, and practiced them in a structured, simulated test-taking environment.

The last step to becoming a "great test taker" is to master the inner mental game of test taking, which centers on maintaining your self-confidence and eliminating self-doubt. By the time you get to this step, you'll realize that you're feeling pretty confident in your ability to rock the exam, and I just want to build on that confidence by going over 2 more strategies—a review of your personal goals, and ignoring the crowd.

Step 1: Remember Your Own Personal Academic Goals and Remember You Achieved Them

This is the hardest step in mastering the mental game of test taking, and you've already done it!

Most students make two big errors: They don't take the time to define their own specific goals in medical school, and they don't study in such a way that they know for sure those goals have been met.

In section I, you got very clear about your own personal goals, and in the process, you were able to trim away a lot of fat, focusing on a very small but important set of information. Then in sections II, III, and IV, you learned a way of finding material to study, and then studying it very efficiently using a strategy that has a clear and defined endpoint.

When your cards are "memorized" they are done, there is no gray area.

You not only limited the amount of information you chose to make cards out of, but you also memorized those cards in record time. Now you can rest assured that you have met your own academic goals before test day. Nothing builds more self-confidence than this.

REMEMBER, that using these methods, you will definitely not know as much material as some of your classmates who studied the entire curriculum and spent 24-7 doing it. But this won't matter to you, because you have different goals, and you succeeded in your own terms.

Furthermore, you know what you know, AND you know what you don't know, because you consciously chose NOT to know that extra stuff. The more confidant you are in your dominance of the material that YOU CHOSE to study, the better you'll do in the game of test taking.

Process: Connecting with Your Personal Goals

Take out the list of goals you made for med school from section I. Now analyze those goals using your knowledge of the system of medical school and residency to figure out your target grade on the test. For example, let's say your goal is to get into your top choice residency in the location and specialty of your choice, and you're preparing for your GI system exam in your second year of medical school.

Then in section II, you learned that the way your schools grading system is set up, the first 2 years are "pass/fail" and you need 70% or above on tests to "pass." Knowing this, your test goal might be to get 75% or 80% to give you some buffer room, because you definitely don't want to fail. As you aim for higher test grades, it takes exponentially more time to get 5% higher. For example, to move from a 65% to 70% might take 2 extra hours of studying, whereas to move from a 95% to 100% might take 200 extra hours of studying. Knowing this, the more clear you are about your target score, given your goals, the more free time you'll have to pursue your goals outside of medical school.

Step 2: Ignore the Crowd

"Did you read Professor Brown's special review notes?"

"I just finished reviewing all of Robbin's path, chapters 4-8, it was soooo helpful!"

"I heard there was a question on the mechanism of praziquantel, did you study that?"

If you haven't already, by the time your first test rolls around, you'll start hearing comments like this. Med students LOVE to stress out together. And the VAST majority of students don't feel prepared for tests—in fact; they feel a bit insecure in their knowledge.

People will say things like this for different reasons. Some feel insecure in what they've been studying and want to get an idea of how much others have done so they know whether they've done enough. Others seem to want to get a leg up on their peers—trying to show off how much they know, and hoping that others will either be intimidated or be grateful to them for helping them out with that last minute information. And then there is that group of students who just have nothing else to talk about, are nervous about the test, and so naturally, start talking about the test.

Regardless of the reason, it's best stay away from these students around test time, or at least to change the subject if they are your friends and you want to hang out. You don't need anyone else's approval to confirm that you're prepared and ready to go for the exam—in contrast to most people, you get that validation INTERNALLY. Also, listening too long to comments like this can throw off your mental game and cause you to doubt yourself, which is the last thing you want before a test. As we talked about earlier, stress, depending on how intense it is, can cut you off from being able to access your memory networks.

Being stressed is almost like being drunk, but instead of soaking your brain with alcohol, you're soaking it with cortisol, epinephrine, and other stress hormones which have the effect of shunting blood and oxygen away from your higher cortical centers and re-directing these vital nutrients to your limbic system and skeletal muscle, literally worsening your ability to think and remember what you studied. If an unavoidable experience of stress occurs, the effect only lasts about 20-30 minutes from the resolution of the stressful experience, so it's not the end of the world. However to the extent possible, avoid activating this stress response anytime near your test time.

One of my best friends used to always wear his iPod to test-day. He'd show up just before the test started, and had his music playing. This way he was not only pumping himself up mentally with songs he liked, but also had a good excuse to stay out of the stress-inducing conversations happening around him. Feel free to copy his technique.

So remember to ignore the crowd, if your buddy read all of Robbins, that's awesome for him, and it does NOT mean you should have done that. Stick with your own goals, and your own INTERNAL validation that you met your goals. Trust yourself that you're more prepared that most, because you are!

Process: Ignore the Crowd

Figure out the best strategies for you to stay away from the people and situations that trigger you to be stressed out and doubt yourself about the test.

For example, you could listen to music while waiting to walk into the test room, or you could change the subject when friends say things that lead you to doubt yourself.

The point is to have strategies that work for you to have unshakable confidence in your own knowledge base.

Chapter 28: Mastering the Logistics of Test Day—Preparing Your Mind and Body for Optimal Functioning

By this point, you have mastered the material, you've practiced the test taking process and found the best strategies that work for you, and you've figured out ways to avoid getting psyched out by your peers. All that's left is the last-minute details of preparing yourself mentally and physically for the test itself...

Pre-Test Prep

- **Get a Good Night's Sleep 2 Days Before Your Test**

    The good news is that your performance on test day is linked to how well you slept TWO DAYS before the test.

    This is incredibly helpful; because you'll almost always have nothing scheduled the day before the test, so let yourself sleep in to your heart's content the evening 2 days before the test. No amount of time studying will be worth the equivalent time you could have spent sleeping that day.

    Also, this means that even if you happen to be a bit stressed out and don't sleep great the actual night before your test, it shouldn't affect your performance too much if you got a good nights sleep the 2 nights before.

- **Only Study the Highest Yield Cards**

    On the day before the test, use your study sessions to study only your highest-level keeper cards (which you made in the "Targeted Review" section above). If you have more time after finishing those, study the next highest level, and so on.

By this point, you may also have additional flashcards you made from your practice tests, or from emailing questions to your professors, so make sure to include those in this final review.

- **Make Your Mind Dump Reference Paper**

    As you're doing this final review, write down on a sheet of paper the information that is highly memorization-intense (things like equations, chromosome numbers, HLA genotypes, pharmacodynamics, etc....).

    Hold onto this paper, you'll be bringing it with you on test day, for a final review just before you walk into take the test. As we discussed earlier in this section, you will essentially load this information into your working memory as you walk into the test, and then "Mind Dump" it onto scratch paper as soon as you are able to in the test room.

- **No New Material**

    At this point, DO NOT try to learn new material. Most of the time, especially if you're reviewing with group study sessions with your friends, you'll realize that there is some material that you don't know inside and out. That is to be expected.

    But do not fall into the trap of trying to learn this, because at this point you don't have enough time to get enough spaced-repetitions in to encode this well into your memory networks. Instead, just recognize and acknowledge that you don't know that subject perfectly, and continue to focus your time and energy on reviewing and mastering the material you do know.

- **Set Up What You Need the Night Before**

    Before going to bed the night before your test, make sure to do whatever you can to lay your mind to rest (i.e. lay out everything you'll need the next morning, set 2 alarms, etc....).

    The goal is that you can rest peacefully knowing everything important is handled and you'll be ready to roll the following morning.

Test Day Tips

- **Prime your Brain**

    Wake up a bit earlier than you usually do to give yourself an hour or so to review some high yield material again. This will get your brain primed and ready for a running start when you get to the test.

- **Fuel the Machine**

    Just to re-cap what you learned in section IV, make sure you give your brain good fuel for the test.

    I recommend eating a breakfast with veggies and about 30 grams of healthy protein (eggs, beans, protein powder, cottage cheese), which will slow down your GI motility so you don't get hungry in the test.

Whatever you do, make sure to avoid high fat/high sugar foods like bread, doughnuts, juices, for the reasons we covered in section IV.

- **Get Pumped Up**

  Just like all pro sports players do before the big game, get yourself pumped up physically and mentally for the test.

  Listen to music, exercise if you have time, do whatever you want that gets you amped for the test.

  You've trained; you've already done the hard work, now it's time to show off your stuff. You should feel excited and ready to dominate the test.

- **Wear Layers**

  The last thing you want is to have the temperature of the room bug you during the test. So wear clothes in layers so you can easily add or take away a layer to stay perfectly comfortable.

- **Stay Confident**

  Do what you need to do to stay out of stressful conversations before the test.

  Either show up at school just before the test starts, or hang out with your close friends who aren't going to talk about school-related things. Or, do what my buddy did and listen to music, whatever works.

- **Encode Your Mind Dump Review Sheet Into Your Short-Term Memory**

About 10 minutes or so before you have to walk into the test, take out that paper of memorization-intensive information you made earlier.

Read it, then close your eyes and try to recall it. Keep doing this over and over, repeating the info in your head as you walk into the test and find your seat.

The Test Itself

In the test itself, just use the same strategies (hopefully habit by now) that worked best for you in practice tests, here is a review:

- Mind Dump
- Pace Yourself
- Prioritize your Questions
- Strategically Read and Highlight the Test Question
- Choose Your Best Answer and Track the Questions you Don't Know
- Systematically Review Your Answers
- Fill Out Your Answer Sheet All at Once at the End of the Test
- Use All Your Time
- Constantly Feed and Re-Fuel Your Brain with Healthy Snacks and the Right Dose of Caffeine.

After the Test

Yes, it's time to celebrate of course. But on your way to the party take a few minutes to think reflect on the test you just took and notice any "system" errors in the way you approached and took the test.

At this point, it's too late to learn information you didn't know, but it's a perfect time to think about and improve upon the WAY you took the test and how that could be improved. What triggers threw off your mental mojo? What were the surprises? Did you pace yourself correctly or did you run out of time? Was the type of information in your mind dump useful and accessible?

Quickly record your answers (I usually just do this with an iPhone voice memo that I know I'll get back to sometime). This can help you with the next test to avoid and correct any "systemic" problems with how you take tests.

Celebrate!

Congratulations! YOU ARE DONE!!!

Hopefully you just rocked your test, and are on your way to getting continually improving results with less and less time and more and more fun in the process!

The Last Chapter: Why I Really Wrote This Book

Something is seriously wrong with our current system for educating doctors in America. It is incredibly difficult to get into medical school. Students must have not only have superb academic performance, but also demonstrated leadership, civic service, communication skills, empathy, and a commitment to social justice. Those who are offered admission to medical school likely could get any job they desire after college, yet they choose to go through a rigorous training program, often going into $200,000 or more of debt, in order to enter a career of helping others in a direct and tangible way.

And yet, the ironic thing is that despite starting with a group of people that are intelligent, compassionate, and empathic, medical school training often leads to a DECREASE in empathy[9]. Not only that, but also there is an ugly growing phenomenon in healthcare workers called "burnout" that encompasses an internal state of emotional exhaustion, depersonalization, and a low sense of personal accomplishment. Studies have shown that burnout affects nearly 50% of medical students[10], up to 75% of residents[11] and continues to affect practicing physicians.

So why is it that the default path to becoming a physician puts us at such high risk for decreased empathy and burnout which can then lead to clinical depression, substance abuse, patient errors, and in the worst cases suicide?

---

[9] Chen D, Lew R, Hershman W, Orlander J. A cross-sectional measurement of medical student empathy. J Gen Intern Med. 2007 Oct; 22(10): 1434-8.
[10] Ishak W, Nikravesh R, Lederer S, Perry R, Ogunyemi D, Bernstein C. Burnout in medical students: a systematic review. Clin Teach. 2013 Aug; 10(4): 242-5.
[11] Ishak WW, Lederer S, Mandili C, Nikravesh R, Seligman L, Vasa M, Ogunyemi D, Bernstein CA. Burnout during residency training: a literature review. J Grad Med Educ. 2009 Dec; 1(2): 236-42.

I believe a big player in this phenomenon is the habits students learn early in their training. When you put a group of top achievers together, tell them to learn an unreasonable amount of information and to spend 4-8 hours a day at school and another 4-8 hours studying, and then grade them on a curve and link their future career goals to their grades, burnout and decreased empathy is an expected result.

In order to attempt to meet these unreasonable goals, well-meaning students including myself will cut back on what might seem like "not essential" activities to make more time for the demands of studying and learning. Many students will spend less time building and maintaining meaningful relationships, spend less time on physical health activities like exercise and healthy eating, and spend less time on on personal hobbies, recreation, and relaxation. As I discussed in section III, through the process of long-term potentiation, the microanatomy of our brains shifts moment to moment based on where we place our attention and what behaviors we repeatedly do. When we start medical with habits of over-working at the expense of our personal wellbeing and committed relationships, and continue these behaviors throughout residency, they become an unconscious "default pathway" of thinking, feeling, and behaving. These are the habits that lead to burnout, dissatisfied physicians, dissatisfied patients, and a higher rate of patient errors.

The real reason I've written his book is to break this cycle at its start. What would happen if, at the beginning of medical training, we learn and practice tools and strategies for highly efficient rapid learning, enjoy the process of learning, and use our newly created free time to nurture our own physical, mental, emotional, and spiritual wellbeing and that of our most committed relationships? I believe that this would have a ripple effect, leading to not only happier and healthier physicians, but also healthier and more satisfied patients.

If you agree, then please practice the strategies you learned in this book, improve upon them, share them with the people you care about, and give me your feedback on my website, www.facebook.com/studycoachmd. And PLEASE, treat your free time as precious and use it with intention to do what you love.

Thank you for your time, your attention, and for your courage to take a risk to create the life you want,

-Dave Larson, MD

198

Gratitude:

Although I may have learned how to learn and memorize quickly by practicing the tools in this book, learning how to write, teach, and consolidate that into a book was a much more difficult task and has been years in the making. I am SO grateful for all of the people who have taught, inspired, supported, and mentored me along the way.

First and foremost, I want to thank the rock star students at USC's Keck School of Medicine who taught me how to optimize my strategies for learning and how to live a balanced life as a med student. My roommates and best buds—Christian, Matt, Coach, Winter, Prez, JB, who reminded me to take myself lightly and provided limitless entertainment during study breaks. And I can forget my mentor-extraordinaire, Dr. Sanchez who continues to inspire me about global health.

To my team at UCSD: My fearless leaders Drs. Zisook, Folsom, Lindeman, Lillie, to the people who really run things, Tracy and Ruben, and to all my incredible co-residents; thank you for all you have done and continue to do to support me in following my dreams. Dr. Bhatti, thank you for teaching me how to be an authentic doctor, and how to work with love and enthusiasm. To all the UCSD Med Students I've met along the way, thank you for teaching me your favorite study techniques and for giving me great feedback on this book.

To Kris King and the team at Wings, thank you for teaching me how to get clear about what I want, how to find the courage to ask for it, and how to think outside of the box to find ways to create it. I can't imagine living life without the tools I've learned from you.

To my mentors who don't know they're my mentors...Paul Farmer—thank you for being my first example of how to do med school differently, and for your incredible service with

Partners in Health. To Tim Ferriss, thank you for teaching me about lifestyle design, how to live better, and how to think big. To Dr. Neha, thank you for teaching me to believe in myself and reminding me of the many ways to be a healer.

To Dr. Ishak and Dr. Moutier, thank you for all the work you to do better understand physician burnout and to promote resilience and wellbeing in our future doctors.

To my patients, thank you for teaching me why I'm doing all of this in the first place, for reminding me about the importance of the human connection in medicine, and for teaching me how much better of a doctor I can be for you when I take care of myself too.

To all my friends, from Moose and Chris in elementary, to the RB crew of fun, all you rock stars at Brown, the team at Keck, and now all you great people in San Diego—Mari, Steve, Cassidy, Rach, and so many more... Thank you all for your support and encouragement, for teaching me how important it is to balance work and play, and for so many great times and memories together.

To my family and new Alfery family, thank you for your incredible generosity, constant cheerleading, and unconditional support of me following my dreams, no matter how much they changed along the way! Paul, the "Tech Daddy," thank you for kicking this off by teaching me how to study with electronic flashcards. Mom and Dad, thank you for showing me how to live a balanced life as a physician and how to maintain joy, enthusiasm, and a deep respect for the opportunity to practice medicine. I want to be like you when I grow up!

And finally to the love of my life Janna, my biggest fan, and my bestest friend. There is no way I could have done this without your constant support, encouragement, and reminding me that done is better than perfect. I love you more than words can express.

About the Author

David Larson, M.D. is an integrative medicine physician, leadership seminar facilitator, and life hacker. He studied business at Brown University before spending a year in Spain on a Fulbright Fellowship and then working in rural India in the public health sector. He then attended USC School of Medicine and graduated with highest distinction, earning the Alpha Omega Alpha merit scholarship. He is currently in his final year of postgraduate medical training at UCSD, pursuing 3 residencies in Family Medicine, Psychiatry, and Integrative Medicine.

Made in the USA
Middletown, DE
20 January 2019